A SELF PUBLISHER'S

COMPANION

EXPERT ADVICE FOR
AUTHORS WHO WANT
TO PUBLISH *from*
TheBookDesigner.com

JOEL FRIEDLANDER

Marin Bookworks

Printed in the United States of America

First Printing, 2011

ISBN 978-0-936385-11-2   Trade paper
ISBN 978-0-936385-12-9   Ebook formats

Marin Bookworks
369-B Third Street #572
San Rafael, CA 94901
www.TheBookDesigner.com

This book is also available in all major ebook formats. For more information and links to retailers, please go to:
www.TheBookDesigner.com/Companion

The article "The Hub & Outpost Method to Organize Your Social Media Marketing" was originally written for CreateSpace, Inc. and is used here with their permission.

Typeset with Adobe InDesign in Adobe Caslon Pro and Chaparral typefaces, both the work of type designer Carol Twombly.

Contents

Preface

I write a blog about book design, e-books, self-publishing and the indie publishing life. Recently I received this comment on an article I wrote over a year ago as part of a series on book construction. It's from a long-time reader:

> "I have a question. What became of the rest of the series? I've been trying to find it, to no avail. I was especially interested in seeing a piece on how to paginate correctly (which was supposed to come after this one). Have I missed some special secret way to get at your archives?"

I understand completely, and I was able to point the reader to the article she was looking for.

I love blogging. It has given me real rewards as a writer, as a small business owner, as a content creator, and as an information marketer.

But I don't love everything about blogging. The programs we use (my blog runs on WordPress) are frequently referred to as content management systems. The WordPress software is a terrific boon to anyone who wants to publish online. It makes it so easy, even I can do it. I've even been able to use WordPress to set up regular websites on my own.

But blogs, by their nature, are organized by chronology. In other words, the thing that characterizes blogs is that the newest articles always appear first, on the home page.

As each new article is published, of course, the older ones are pushed down one notch. If you publish a post every day, the way I do, after a month there are 30 other posts on top of that great article you wrote last month. Next month there will be 60 posts to dig through to get to it.

We try to overcome this basic infrastructure with tags and categories and sneeze pages and popular post widgets and lots of other gadgets, but they can only help so much. You can't turn a blog into a structured, hierarchical website no matter what you do with your tags and categories.

So, with 450 articles in my archive (and growing) there's a lot of valuable information that gets buried under the pile of more recent posts. And that's why I started looking for ways to dig these posts out and create a book from them.

Over a period of a few weeks I was able to come up with a system to process this large amount of information. I hoped to find a book in my blog archives, and eventually, I did.

I write a lot of articles about practical, detailed, nuts-and-bolts kind of things you need to know to design, produce, market and sell your book, but you'll find very little of that here.

Because there are several terrific books on the market that explain all the steps you need to take to succeed as a self-publisher, I saw no need to add another one to the pile.

Instead of a how-to book, I decided to create a kind of "why-to" book. In *A Self-Publisher's Companion* I've pulled together the writing I think is the best I've done on the world of self-publishing today. I hope it will be a real companion to authors thinking about getting into the exciting and fast-changing world of self-publishing.

Joel Friedlander
San Rafael, February, 2011

Introduction

This book lies at the confluence of two of the biggest changes in the media landscape of the written word: self-publishing and blogging.

Self-Publishing, an American Tradition

Publishing your own book without intermediaries has a long and erratic tradition in the United States. Examples of early self-publishers are largely irrelevant, since the modern notion of self-publishing depends on the opposition of this type of book publishing to traditional publishing. In the dominant form of publishing, publishers acquire rights to literary properties, improve and complete the transition of the property from a manuscript to a book, from raw materials to a consumer product.

They then advertise, market, promote and sell the products of their efforts, while paying the creator of the original manuscript a rather small percentage of their revenue as a royalty. The creator is an equity partner in the enterprise of the book, but a decidedly junior partner. The author is at the mercy of the contract she has signed, the scruples of the publisher she has signed with, and the vagaries of the marketplace, about which she may know nothing, since the entire structure and mechanism of publishing keeps writers isolated from both their readers and the ways that publishers actually work.

In opposition to this, or sometimes parallel to the track of traditional publishing but largely unknown to it, there have always been authors who, for whatever reason, did not participate in this whole mechanism. Perhaps they objected to the publishers acting as gatekeepers who only allow a certain few writers into the world of published authors. If you didn't have what the publisher or his agents wanted, you didn't get published.

Some authors chose vanity publishers, companies that are not truly publishers at all, but who sell services and books to their own authors, who are, in reality, their true customers.

But many other writers set up publishing companies of their own, and became true self-publishers. They obtained ISBNs from Bowker, listed themselves in various directories, established discount schedules and distribution plans and acted in every way just like traditional publishers, but only published the works of one author—themselves.

And Some Personal History

When I decided to self-publish in the 1980s, it was still a time when self-publishers were looked on as third-class citizens, not truly members of the publishing industry. Consequently, like many other self-publishers, I made lots of efforts to appear to be an actual small independent publisher. Various family members were listed as officers in the company, and correspondence was sent out over the signature of someone who was not the author of the only book on our list. We used a post office box at the Grand Central Postal Station on Lexington Avenue in New York for our mailing address. Even the name of the press was generic—Globe Press

Books—and designed to evoke associations of other, better known publishing houses.

I followed the advice and gained from the encouragement of Dan Poynter, whose *Self-Publishing Manual* became my bible. My books were typeset by real typesetters I knew in New York, and printed by real book printers. And while there were always self-publishers who were successful, who took a businesslike approach to publishing, it remained a sideline, and an unloved stepchild of the publishing indsutry.

So What Changed?

Today the picture is radically different in some ways, maddeningly the same in others. But over all, the entire world of self-publishing has been yanked out of the shadow of the conglomerate publishers by technological innovation.

First, print on demand, using digital printing, revolutionized book printing and distribution by eliminating the need to print—and pay for—thousands of books just to gain entree to the publishing world.

By eliminating the risk associated with an investment of $10,000 or more, print on demand allowed the tens of thousands of people who had always dreamed of publishing a book to do so at almost no upfront cost.

Companies have sprung up to take advantage of the ease of publishing with this technology, and sometimes to take advantage of the authors who rushed to fulfill their dreams. We now have another category of companies, subsidy publishers, to account for this development. Sometimes erroneously referred to as "self-publishing companies," these firms occupy a position somewhere between vanity publishers and book printers, who don't claim to be publishers at all, even though they may offer services similar to the functions once found only inside a traditional publishing company.

Blogging, Another Form of Self-Publishing

The other technological innovation that has changed publishing is the widespread adoption of the internet. When we finally gained the ability to create a two-way interaction with this powerful new media, the social network was born.

The first social media was blogging, a form of posting articles to websites that's easy enough even for writers to do it. But what made blogging social was the function built into blogging software that allowed readers to take part in the conversation, to interact directly with the writer by commenting on the articles she was writing.

The interactive nature of blogging, and then of other social media innovations, is changing many aspects of our life. But blogging itself has continued to grow and adapt to widely different contexts and means of delivering information, entertainment and opinion to interested readers. And while blogs have grown to include audio and video, they are still predominantly text.

Two results of the continuing rise of blogging as a media activity of importance in our culture have been reinforcing the primacy of text and reading to the online experience, and reinforcing the importance of writers as influencers. Text dominates the web, and writers produce that text. The writing that makes a difference in people's lives, that causes mass movements, or that sells huge numbers of products are from the keyboards of copywriters, journalists, bloggers, enthusiasts, and passionate followers of a cause.

Things Come Together

When I started blogging in late 2009 there was already a rich landscape of publishing blogs, book blogs, review blogs and, of course, technology blogs without end.

But there was little that I could find that talked about self-publishing as a part of the long tradition of bookmaking, about the design of books as an intrinsic part of how books are positioned, marketed and sold. And a lack of many of the basic book-building skills that self-publishers need to create professional-level books.

So TheBookDesigner.com was born. I tried to find the subjects that would be of the most interest to potential readers who were interested in this whole new world of personal, do-it-yourself book making. And people responded. Articles about typography, about type design, book layout, copyright, about the minutia of publishing like how to decipher bar codes, they all found readers.

It's rewarding when you've spent most of your life pursuing a field that's unknown to the average person to all of a sudden wake up to a whole world of readers who want to know those arcane bits of knowledge and who are eager to read your next article. As a writer, it's damned rewarding. Instead of boring family and friends with nuances of type design, I could talk to people who were actually interested.

As I've continued to blog and to interact with the lively and educated community that takes part in conversations on my blog, I've learned a lot. Now the talk is all about ebooks, the technology that will cause the next big shift in book publishing.

Throughout the time I've been blogging, it has become apparent to me how much blogging has in common with self-publishing, and the happy confluence of these two ideas in my own life.

They really are very similar, don't you think? Blogging is, in fact, a subset of self-publishing as far as I'm concerned. Like a bridge between the printed books of the past and the electronic books of the future, blogging puts the power of the media in the hands of an individual, so that a guy sitting in his spare bedroom in San Rafael, California, can write an article on any subject that interests him and have it read by people all over the world within hours. And then enter into an ongoing conversation with those readers about the ideas and practices contained in that article.

This scenario presents me with most of the results I hoped to get from self-publishing all those years ago, and in a more immediate and interactive way. Truly, it is a golden age for self-publishing of every kind.

Unlike self-publishing, in which we intentionally create a manuscript for a book, taking care to make it consistent, readable and cohesive, blogs are made up of bits and pieces of ideas, often written in the context of a particular moment in time.

This book is an attempt to solve that problem.

On the one hand, it was created with you in mind. I went through the archives of my blog looking specifically for articles that contained my best advice for new self-publishers. I ignored the articles that dealt with specific tools like writing software or page layouts. I ignored the many articles about specific practices in book design and production, since there will be other places for those in future books. And I eliminated articles that were reviews, link collections, and news of the day posts.

I wanted to find, and to offer to you, the articles that would come together to give you an overview of the self-publishing possibilities we have available today, to warn you of mistakes that are easy to avoid if you only know about them, and to encourage you to use these tools to pursue the publication of your ideas, your history, your dreams, and your personal story.

I am a self-publishing advocate. The fact that many self-published books are unreadable, dreadful to look at, or otherwise flawed, means nothing to me. I applaud them all. Each book represents a writer reaching out to share something of herself with the wider world. Each has a readership, no matter how small. And for every hundred dreadful books, there will be gems, transformative reading experiences, practical knowledge you can't find anywhere else, or life changing memoirs that amaze us.

So my message to you is: go out and publish, make your voice heard, spread your word in the world. It's all good.

A Self-Publishing
Orientation

Why Self-Publishing is Entering a Golden Age

Whenever a discussion about self-publishing gets heated, you can be sure someone will say, "If we let just anybody publish a book, soon we'll be buried in bad, unedited books and all the good ones will be lost in a sea of crap!"

There were over 350,000 books published in the United States last year, more than ever. And that doesn't include the hundreds of thousands of books moved to print on demand servers and assigned ISBNs, and therefore "published."

I don't feel buried, do you? Where are all those books? Apparently, it's not that easy to find them. You have to actually make an effort. You won't get drowned in some tsunami of badness, you have to go looking and jump in.

The Real Shame of It All

Writers who are waiting for the gatekeeper to come and welcome them into the promised land behind the gates may have a long wait ahead of them, and that's too bad.

You know why? Because we're about to enter a real golden age of self-publishing. There is no denying the fact that a whole lot of people have something to say and are busy writing their books. They want to publish, put their thoughts, their history, their research, their story into the arena, and why not?

It might seem overblown to call it a golden age, but I think it's really happening, and here's why:

The playing field is leveling—Net neutrality ensures the internet stays equally available to all. As far as online business is concerned, each book competes on its own. In this environment it's your passion, persistence and pluck that will sell your book, and those are all within your control.

There is easy access to tools and professionals—In order to make top-quality books, you need people with top-quality skills. Part of the downsizing of the publishing industry has been the upsizing of the freelance marketplace, where every talent you need to build a superior book is available.

Social media marketing—The person-to-person communication that typifies social media can be scaled up through the intelligent use of socially-enabled websites where your readers congregate. When you get involved in social media you can begin to build a community based on your personality and your ability to communicate, not on huge advertising budgets. Social media, blogging, forums all drive traffic and can make your book a success outside normal promotional channels.

Elimination of production risk—Digital printing and print on demand distribution have eliminated almost all of the production risk of publishing. Book printing, storage and fulfillment are the biggest costs of traditional publishing and this new system makes it possible to get into print for almost nothing. It's now cheaper to publish a book than to copy one at Kinko's.

Prejudices are starting to crack—More authors are moving to e-books, and e-books are even easier to self-publish than print books. The attraction of 70% royalties is strong, of course, but so is the ability to control your own publication, something that's long been denied to authors. Publishers have given over more responsibility to authors to build their own platform, to do a lot of their own marketing. But this has also empowered authors to take the autonomy and exercise real choices over their own publications.

The softening definition of books—We are in the beginning of a transition to e-books, although print books look like they have plenty of life left in them. Book traditions of hundreds of years are still strong, and this may be one of the last times most people in the world will have learned to read from books printed on paper. Books are already beginning to stretch and change, and e-book markets are as friendly to new forms and formats for text as they are to digital texts that are made to look like "books." All kinds of writing and information products will find life electronic forms that were simply uneconomical to produce before.

The globalizing force of the internet—E-books and apps have opened the world market to books in electronic form without regard to national boundaries, an unprecedented development in publishing that will continue to grow with the adoption of these new forms.

Mobile technology—The spread of mobile computing technology has increased the amount of reading in the world. Now we read everywhere, and the digitization of books into e-books and apps has opened the whole world of smart phones, tablets, MP3 players, and other devices to books, a phenomenon that has never existed before. The average smartphone user can now carry in her pocketbook a massive library that would have dwarfed entire home libraries just a few years ago. And there are over 50 million smartphones in use around the world.

That's my list. I think we've only seen the beginning of the curve, and it's heading up.

Habits of Successful Self-Publishers

I'll bet you know people who are very happy at their jobs, who like the company they work for, who have worked to get into a good position there and are pleased to be able to continue their employment.

Sure you do, but they aren't self-publishers. No, authors who take the leap into self-publishing are cut from a different cloth. They are restless, they might have something to prove, they may have a message for humanity, or a record they want to leave behind. Whatever it is, they have a passion for their subject, the drive to communicate it, and the belief that there are people waiting to hear it.

See if you recognize yourself here. Successful self-publishers are:

Proactive—By definition, self-publishers are people willing to take charge and make something happen, otherwise they would still be waiting for a letter from an agent. Beyond that, self-publishers are entrepreneurs who are on the lookout for new sales opportunities, new communities that might be interested in their books, new opportunities to bring their message, whatever it may be, to a larger public.

The market—Self-publishers most often come from the fields they are writing about. As experts in their fields, they also entered the market as newcomers and had to learn how to succeed in that field. This gives them the ability to speak to today's newcomers—the biggest market in any niche.

Research-driven—Although authors are enthusiastic and passionate about their subject matter, successful self-publishers use research to find the questions that are being asked most frequently. No matter how they started out in self-publishing, success has taught them to follow the market, to find ways to stay in touch with the trends and influencers in their field. Whether it's with keyword research, marketing studies, or direct mail tests, they continuously try to find the best way to bring their books to market.

Financially conservative—Controlling costs is important for all businesses, and successful self-publishers husband their resources, spending only where it will produce the biggest effect. They know what it costs to publish a book. Success demands leveraging resources, and not trying to act like a big publisher with a multimillion dollar advertising and promotion budget. The successful self-publisher is more likely to have *Guerrilla Marketing* on her bedside than advertising rate sheets.

Experts—Most successful nonfiction self-publishing teaches something. Successful self-publishers know that they don't have to be an expert on everything, but within their chosen specialty they ought to be extremely knowledgeable. Sometimes this takes the form of becoming an expert for newcomers, because that's possible for anyone who has already passed the early stages of their career. New people in any field usually buy most of the how-to material that's perfect for self-publishing.

Persistent—Becoming a self-publisher is in every way like becoming an entrepreneur, or starting a small business, or taking up internet marketing. Whatever the path, starting something new takes guts and persistence. There will be times when you feel like nothing is working, and you don't understand anything. Successful self-publishers, almost by definition, are people who have kept on going, adapted when necessary, but never doubted they would reach their goals.

Marketers—Some authors become self-publishers because they are recognized experts, or to enhance their standing in their field, or to justify an increase in their fees. Some because they are committed to a cause, or have a story that just has to "get out" and this is the only way they can do it. But all successful self-publishers share a marketer's sensibility. They are attuned to the needs of their audience and find profitable ways to fill those needs.

Some people become successful as they go along. Some have a few of these strong traits, and pick up others as needed. Self-publishing can be a folk art, learned by individuals through trial and error. It's the determination to go forward, and to focus on their audience, that most sets them apart.

I'll tell you something else: I have a copy of this list on my wall. It's not that any one of us can be all these things, but when I read it I know I want to keep going. How about you?

"I Want to Be a Book Publisher"

I was talking with a self-publisher today about everything he had learned over the months spent getting his book ready to go to press.

It had been a long haul putting the book together, and the author had worked with several editors before asking me to help him put the project together.

"Well," he said, "I've got my publishing company all set up. Maybe I'll make it into a real publishing company. Publish books for other authors who are just starting out." I could see this was an idea with some charm to it.

I was a little surprised at this, since the book hadn't even gone on sale yet. There's nothing quite like the experience of taking delivery on 1,000 or 2,000 hardcovers and wondering if you'll ever see the money that went into them again.

That's when you know whether you want to be a book publisher, and whether you have a gift for it.

"How will you do that?" I asked. "Are you going to publish only books in your niche?"

"Look, I've learned how books get put together, how they get edited, designed, typeset and how to get printing quotes and arrange for fulfillment and all the rest. If you don't have to learn all that, there's some value there, isn't there? That's what publishers do, after all." He seemed satisfied with this.

Storms on the Horizon

But I sensed something was missing.

"Not really," I said. "Publishers have a market. There's some group of people they are tuned into and know well. What they do is go out and find the books that their market wants to buy. Publishers are media companies. They risk their own money on properties they think their market will buy in enough quantity that they'll make a profit.

"If they publish business books, it's the business community. If it's cookbooks, they are selling to home cooks. It's their connection to the market that's critical, that makes the company. Editing, book design, the other nuts and bolts are secondary to their business, really."

He was looking quizzical by now.

"On the other hand," I went on, "if you charge authors for arranging their publication, getting their ISBNs, having their books edited, designed, and put into distribution, you are no longer a media company. Now you're an author-services company, or a subsidy publisher.

"Your market is made up of aspiring authors and self-publishers. Your profitability will have nothing to do with your ability to find and cultivate writers who appeal to your market, because you will publish anyone who can pay the freight. You no longer have to sell books at all to be profitable. You only have to sell services to authors.

"These are two completely different kinds of companies. Which one did you mean, when you said you wanted to be a publisher?" We looked at each other and smiled.

"I guess I'll have to think about that one, Joel," he said, and we went on with our business.

Two Kinds of Self-Publishers— Which One Are You?

As a new blogger on book design and self-publishing, but an old hand at helping authors publish their books, I've been treated to quite a tour of the virtual world the last few weeks.

One of the first things I noticed were the numerous, on-going, and passionate arguments about self-publishing itself; is it the "best idea ever," or does it simply make you "want to cringe," both comments I found in recent days.

There's also quite a bit of confusion about self-publishing and arguments that seem fueled principally by semantic disagreements or misinformation.

Two Kinds of Self-Publishers

It seems a lot easier to understand if you realize that there are two types of self-publishers (and yes, this is a generalization, but hopefully a useful one).

"Hobby" Publisher—This is someone who may be writing a cookbook for the PTA, a memoir to share with family members, a photographer creating a book to commemorate an event, a poet wanting to finally see her poems in print, or a novelist tired of the rejections from traditional publishing houses. The common denominator is that they expect the exercise to cost them money, as any hobby would. They publish to fulfill a personal need, or for an institutional reason.

In a way, it's difficult to call these activities "publishing" because publishing implies making a work available to the public. One thing we can say with assurance is that few of these books will be seen by anyone outside the author's circle of family, friends and colleagues. From reports in the press, it seems that these books will have virtually no sales outside of those closed circles.

This person may not know what an ISBN is and, in most cases, have no reason to know. They may not know that the odd-numbered pages of books are always on the right-hand side, or how the book distribution system works. They are mostly price-sensitive and pleased to find out there's a website that will "publish" their book for nothing. They may have no interest in copy editing, proofreading, indexing, and the like. They want a book, and now they can have one.

Consequently, the way these books are made, the suppliers who cater to these self-publishers, and the standards applied to these books (basically, none) are actually quite appropriate for the intentions of the "publisher." These are the people that all the so-called "self-publishing websites" are intended to serve. It might be more accurate to characterize these companies as manufacturers because essentially they are producing products for a customer, almost exclusively sold to the customer's account.

"Competitive" Self-Publisher—This self-publisher knows that publishing their own book also means that they are going into business. They may be a previously published author trying to break into a new niche, a consultant publishing a book on their specialty or, more likely, a nonfiction author of a niche book who has the entrepreneurial spirit to

realize that they can make their book a financial success all by themselves.

This type of self-publisher has been around a long time, and predates the print on demand era, although print on demand has lowered the risk for these publishers and encouraged them to bring new books to market.

This self-publisher has done her homework. If she intends to sell her books in bookstores, she knows she will have to compete with books from conglomerate publishers for space. Often an enthusiast or recognized expert in the field they write in, they may already have an audience for their book from their own activities.

This publisher will hire professionals to edit, design, lay out and produce her book, and will more than likely have professional marketing help as well. She will follow a production schedule, or find a competent *book shepherd* to organize the myriad details of production, distribution and launch. She will form a company and will publish her book as a business activity. She expects, like any businessperson, to make a profit. For some authors, the profit from publication is most important, but in other cases the prestige, leverage, or enhanced speaking and lecturing opportunities are the expected profit.

Both Kinds of Self-Publishers Can Be Successful

I've produced wonderful books for both kinds of self-publishers. Many of the books published by a "competitive" self-publisher, given an author who is motivated and attentive to business, go on to make money. Self-publishing niche nonfiction, especially for someone known in their field, is almost always profitable. Dan Poynter has been launching self-publishers like this for many years.

I've often asked prospective clients to tell me how they would define "success" for their publishing project. The answer to this question determines everything that follows. Listening carefully to your own answer to this question will guide you through the thickets of self-publishing. Good luck.

Seven Scenarios for Successful Self-Publishing

I've often been asked these questions: Why would a writer want to self-publish? And what kind of work is especially suited to self-publishing?

Because I've been involved in launching self-publishers since the 1990s, when I hear these questions I immediately start to think of the many authors I've met and the ones for whom I've produced books. These authors stand out for me because I'm drawn to their personalities, histories and the reasons they became self-publishers.

Without identifying them by name, each of their situations speak to the many reasons people decide to publish themselves, and to what effect Here are seven of the authors I've produced books for, and the reasons they brought to their own publication.

Genre switcher—This client was a professional author who had published a string of nonfiction books with major publishers. But his dream was to write a contemporary thriller and sell it to the movies. Unfortunately, no one would look at the book, and told him he should stick to nonfiction. Determined to prove them wrong, he mounted a major effort to edit, print and market his book.

A long shot from beginning to end, the book never sold, although it was certainly no worse than many genre novels published more traditionally. But the client was satisfied he had made his point.

Educational consultant—A woman who was quite well known as a consultant to educators wanted to create a book that embodied her philosophy of education, something that would inspire teachers. She felt it would not be published according to her vision by a commercial publisher, and so she created the book herself and sold it through her own consulting company.

The book came out beautifully, obviously a labor of love, and the consultant had both a contribution she made to her field, and a tool to help market her consulting work.

Self-proclaimed guru—It's a dirty world out there. This man controlled a couple of thousand followers, and had developed his own rather bizarre system of philosophy. No publisher would be interested in the book, yet the guru and his followers sincerely felt it was a "gift to humanity" and spared no expense to put it into print.

The publication of the book, even though it was read by virtually no one outside the group, seemed to give the guru even more authority in the eyes of his followers.

Poet—Although it's notoriously difficult to get a publishing contract for an unknown author, there's really nothing to compare to trying to get into print if you're a poet. This poet, acclaimed and published in numerous anthologies, knew the only way he would ever get published was to do it himself. He set up a company, we published the book, and it opened numerous doors to him.

The satisfaction of having the book to both sell and share with friends and colleagues was very gratifying, and the poet gained a lot of knowledge about publishing that will be useful later on.

Exercise innovator—An innovative thinker in the field of therapeutic exercise, this client was building himself as a brand in a calculated and entrepreneurial way. An integral part of his multi-faceted plan was the publication of a book demonstrating his own theories and exercises, with lots of drawing and explanations of his system.

This author had strong business instincts. He was marketing himself agressively, had a definite plan in mind, and used the book as a building block in his assault on success.

Political theorist—Political theories are often impossible to get published. The very small market is difficult to penetrate. This author had been publishing his own books for years and had built a following of several thousand fans through his speaking and writing activities. He knew exactly what to pay, how many to print, and how to sell these books to his audience.

As part of an ongoing business model, the author's book publishing perfectly complemented the deep thought and rigorous analysis for which he was known.

Retired professor—After a long career teaching anthropology, this professor finally had time to put together the book he had always dreamed of writing. Because he chose an unusual form—half straight science and half an imagined, fictional narrative—the book was unsaleable. He published himself to fulfill the dream.

The author went on to publish several more books of a similar style and, although sales were negligible, he had great enjoyment in creating and publishing books that expressed his ideas exactly the way he wanted.

It's All About Knowing Where You Are

I admit I enjoy doing these books. Whether the books are "good" or not seems not as relevant to me as the fact that these authors believed strongly in what they had to say, and wrested control of the means to launch their ideas into the world. I kind of admire that, don't you?

Each had definite reasons that made a lot of sense to them. None had come to the decision easily, although the more entrepreneurial authors always seem much less burdened by the idea that they were becoming "authors." For them it just made good business sense, and so they did it.

With writers, the motives for writing are so different from person to person. To bring that vision to the rest of the world through publishing is, in many ways, an entirely natural thing to do. It's an extension of the initial drive to write, the desire to communicate, because where there's a writer, there also needs to be a reader to truly complete the process. Publishing is, in a simple way, just that: a way to find the readers that every author knows are out there.

And bravo to every one of them.

Each author who decides to self-publish has a logic all his own. Some books may be more profitable than others, but in my experience this is not what moves authors to publish. The more you understand your own motives and goals, the more likely you are to succeed in self-publishing, because you will more accurately define that "success" for yourself.

The Self-Publisher's Self-Questionnaire

I talk to writers every week who are thinking about self-publishing. It's a major step, and each person takes that step in their own way. People seem to be most influenced by their own professional background, and sometimes by knowing someone who published a book.

A big part of my job in these talks is asking questions, trying to see how far into the process they are. Over the years I've been working with self-publishers, I've gradually simplified the questions I ask. One of the best things that comes out of these talks is a clearer picture of the issues they are facing. I try to put the pieces together, show how they fit, when everything seems confusing and disjointed.

Publishing a book is pretty complex. The problem is that we take books for granted. Most of us have been reading from the time our parents or early teachers could get us started. They read to us, made sure there were books in the house. Books are so common, such everyday objects that we don't realize everything that goes into them until we have to make all these decisions ourselves. Then it starts to get complicated pretty fast.

If you're thinking about self-publishing and you've never done it, you can have a little "consulting call" with yourself. I've cooked down the gist of my talks with authors into the following nine questions. So go ahead and interview yourself. Try to answer as if we're sitting across a table from each other at Peet's Coffee in San Rafael.

Questions, Questions, Questions

1. *How do you feel about starting a business (or expanding your business, if you already have one)?* A big misconception about self-publishing is that it's all about literary fulfillment, self-validation or artistic expression. Very soon you will learn that publishing is a business, complete with the need to keep records, pay taxes, organize a business structure and many other details of business life. It isn't any more complicated than many other home-based businesses, but it isn't any less complicated either. What's your attitude toward business? How do you feel about marketing? Does it fill you with excitement, the thrill of the hunt, or make you want to hide under the covers?

2. *What would make you feel the publication of your book was a "success"?* Do you have realistic expectations for your book and your publishing company? Is the only measure of success a movie deal, a seat on Oprah's couch, your mug in *People* magazine? Those outcomes are pretty unlikely, no matter who you are. Can you define what would make you feel successful? Is it a number of books sold, or getting a book review in a particular publication? The last time I calculated, I think the New York *Times* reviews about 2,500 books a year. Out of 400,000 or so? This one is crucial, so give it some thought.

3. *Is it essential that you see your book on the bookshelf of retail bookstores?* Another big one. The majority of self-

publishers today are publishing almost exclusively for online sales. The difficulty of getting into bookstores, and the reality of what it actually takes to run a national marketing campaign that would drive people to stores looking for your book put this option out of reach of most people. Exceptions are genres that are served by specialty bookstores where it might be easier to get on the shelf than in general interest or chain stores. If you decide to go for bookstore distribution, it will influence many of the decisions you make while preparing and producing your book. For example you'll certainly need to have the book edited by a professional and you'll need to pay for a real book cover design and at least a serviceable interior. You'll be selling at a deep discount and facing an uphill battle looking for acceptance. You'll need reviews, media kits, some kind of launch to let people know your book is out there. And of course, you will have to solve the number one problem that keeps self-published books out of bookstores to begin with: lack of distribution.

4. *Are you sure you don't want a traditional publisher?* In other words, are you excited about publishing your own book, or are you on the rebound? Feeling rejected by your lover? Want to get even, show them what you've got? Hey, none of these are wrong reasons to self-publish, but ask yourself just how far those emotions will get you. Six months or a year from now, will you still be feeling the same way?

5. *Can you identify or contact a niche group of people interested in your topic?* Nonfiction self-publishing is easier to

get started in if you already know your target audience. Ideally, you are yourself a member of the target audience. You have a community you're a part of, or you're an expert in your field, or you already have a public eager for your writings. It can't be overstated how big a difference this support can make when you're trying to get traction for your book.

6. *Have you thought about what kind of self-publisher you'll be?* Are you a do it yourselfer, or someone who wants to market and sell only online, or a publisher determined to compete with the big boys? Do you intend to do most of the preparation work yourself? Are you determined to learn how to typeset your own book? This question relates directly to the answers you gave to questions 1. and 3. above. If you want to sell in the bookstores and garner reviews for your book, you'll need to approach publishing with both the determination to get the help you need to create a professional book and the budget to pay for it. Remember, this is a business. These expenses are investments in a product with—in many cases—a very long shelf life.

7. *Do you have a plan to learn the nuts and bolts of publishing?* If you plan to hire professionals the whole way, your task will be easier, although you still need to know how to hire the right people for your project. But all the rest of the details of publishing will be up to you. How will you learn about discounts, shipping, print on demand, and all the other needs of your new publishing business? A good place to start might be getting a copy of Dan Poynter's *Self-Publishing Manual* or Sue

Collier and Marilyn Ross' *The Complete Guide to Self-Publishing*, or one of the other comprehensive books on self-publishing.

8. *Are there other books, products or services you can sell once your book is established?* Since you're now the head of a company, you need more products to sell. It's very inefficient to go to all the expense and trouble of setting up your company and learning a new business if you will only have one product. Most successful self-publishers quickly realize they can multiply their efforts and gain profitability much faster by developing new products or services. A series of books, a workbook to accompany a text, a service based on the area of expertise you've demonstrated by publishing your book—these are all good candidates for expanding your "product line."

9. *Do you have a "fire in the belly?"* Publishing a book yourself and trying to sell it can be a tough job. There's a lot to learn, and like most businesses, it takes a while to see results. One thing you can't buy is motivation. Be honest with yourself. Are you excited about self-publishing? Are you just beside yourself waiting to see your book in print? Are you obsessing about marketing plans, scheming how to get book reviews, figuring out how to pay for an editor? These are all good signs. You'll need that drive to see you through to your new life as a self-publisher author.

How did you do? Taking an honest assessment of yourself and your skills before self-publishing can be revealing and helpful in the long run.

Four Ways to Publish Your Book

Okay, you've sweated over your manuscript, you're finished with your re-writes, and it's time to leave the dark of the writer's solitude for the bright wide open world of readers just waiting for your book. But how will you get your book into print? How will you *publish?*

Not so long ago, "getting published" meant one thing and one thing only. You would somehow find a way to get a contract from a publishing house—probably located in New York City—and then wait for them to create a book from your manuscript.

This was never an easy task and, with the consolidation in the book publishing industry, continues to become more difficult with each passing year.

But now there are more options than ever. Before you take the first step down the road to publication, perhaps you should look at the map, and see exactly where that road divides, and where the path you've decided to follow will lead you. To help you choose your path, here are the four basic (very simplified, to be sure) options you have to get "published."

Traditional Publishing

Most books produced by traditional publishing houses are brought to them by literary agents, and many acquisition editors prefer to deal with agents on all acquisition matters. For the prospective author, then, the chief task becomes acquiring an agent who understands the book, has had experience with the market for which the book is intended, maintains contacts with the relevant editors who publish for that market, who has integrity when dealing with authors, and who will arrange a sale to a publisher that benefits the author.

Unfortunately, there are far fewer agents than there are publishing houses, or acquisitions editors. This means that it can be an arduous task to find an agent to represent you and your book. By far the best way to meet an agent who might be a good fit for you is to be referred by one of their successful authors. This is not as rare as you might think, and if you have good contacts within your field, it pays to pursue this avenue.

Traditional publishers will offer a contract and perhaps an advance against the eventual royalties your book will earn. Depending on how the contract is worded—and there are big variations in these matters—you will receive somewhere between 8% and 12% of either the retail price or the wholesale price.

You will have to give up the reproduction rights to the book, and you may be required to release the electronic, first subsidiary, foreign translation, and other rights to the publisher. You may or may not have any control over the development of the manuscript and the final look of the finished book. The publisher will decide how to market the book, and will rely on you, your contacts, and your own marketing efforts as an intrinsic part of the marketing plan for your book.

They will attempt to distribute the book as widely as feasible, and may be able to place your book—if appropriate—into thousands of bookstores around the country, and create public relations opportunities with major media. The publisher will decide when your book no longer warrants any efforts to market it, and may put it out of print within one to two years of initial publication, depending on the sales your book has achieved.

Recommendation: *If you believe your book can be a large-scale block-buster, that Hollywood directors will line up to option your book, or you have already been on* Oprah, *this is the path for you.*

Cooperative Publishing

Although not as well known as other avenues to getting into print, the cooperative publishing model has a lot to recommend it for the right book. Publishers who produce books cooperatively rarely advertise that fact, but it can be a good model for the right book and the right publisher, one in which both profit from the book's publication.

In this model, a publisher who is already issuing books in your market, and who knows how to sell to that market, may offer you a contract different from the normal publishing contract. They will be interested in books that complement their existing line, and will have pretty high standards in both content and writing style for the kinds of books they will consider.

You will be asked to pay a *publication fee* to cover some of the publisher's upfront expenses and, when the books are printed, you will be asked to pay the printer's invoice. In exchange for this investment—and these fees and printing costs can typically run to $5,000–20,000 or more—the publisher will take over all the functions that a traditional publisher provides.

In addition, rather than receive a royalty, you become the equity partner with the publisher in the profits generated by your book. So instead of 8% or 10% of the retail price, you might earn 50% of the net profit. This arrangement removes the financial risk for the publisher, since all costs are substantially covered by the author, and it gives you the cachet and the editorial, production, and marketing capacities of the publishing house.

As an author you will still be responsible for helping to market your book but, with your equity participation, this is much more like a business venture for you. You can justify spending more time and money to sell your book.

Recommendation: *If you are a nonfiction author in a specific niche, and you can identify smaller publishers who aggressively service your field, you may find a great fit with one of those publishers, allowing you to concentrate on writing and selling your book, leaving everything else up to your publishing partner.*

Subsidized or "Vanity" Publishing

In this publishing model, you pay to have your book published. Although you might pay a fee to a Cooperative Publisher, you and the publisher become partners in the success of the book. With subsidized publishing, you pay for a service only, since the company you will deal with has no need to actually sell any books. Their profits are derived only from authors, and this is why they have traditionally been known as "vanity" publishers.

You will contract with a company that may appear to be a traditional publisher, or with one of the ever-sprouting "self-publishing" websites. These companies follow two basic models; either you will pay a fee for the design, typesetting and production of your book, or you will pay a high price for any copies of the book you purchase.

In addition, you will be offered numerous "packages" of services including manuscript editing, marketing, premium interior or cover design, press release mailings, listings in industry directories, illustration, and so on. Each extra service will accrue an additional fee, and these fees can quickly add up to thousands of dollars.

When your book is printed, you will receive somewhere between 1 and 25 copies of the book, although the publisher may claim to print more that they are "holding" against future demand.

Most of the website-centered publishing services companies that offer these services also claim to distribute your book with the aim of furnishing copies to eventual buyers through "print on demand" technology. However, this distribution usually amounts to a listing in a database and nothing more (unless, of course, you purchase an additional "package").

Since these companies derive all their profit from authors, there are no barriers to acceptance. The actual work of these companies is much easier to understand if you think of them more as manufacturers than publishers, and yourself more as a customer than as an author.

Books produced through this option may be well written, or they may be trash. It makes no difference to the subsidy publisher since they are actually just manufacturing products, not publishing *per se*.

Recommendation: *If you would like to print up copies of a cookbook for gifts or fund-raising, or print a book solely for distribution within your company and you have the staff to do it well, this can be a viable option. As with all manufacturing, ignore the hype and compare on price.*

Self-Publishing

Simply put, this path to publication is when the author decides to also become the publisher of his book.

As such, the author will form a publishing company of his own. He will obtain his own ISBN range, so book databases will recognize his company as the publisher of the book. The author now becomes responsible for all the functions usually provided by the publisher.

The author will need to provide—or contract for—editorial, interior and cover design, proofreading, illustration, indexing, proofing and manufacturing, warehousing if books are produced by offset printing, order fulfillment and shipping, accounting, marketing, publicity and sales. The author has gone from a lone worker in front of a screen, to a replacement for a multi-function, complex business designed to acquire, create, produce, and sell a product.

To address this daunting challenge the self-published author will need to educate herself about all the areas mentioned above, and will need to become familiar with the practices of the publishing industry and the bookselling trade. She will need to learn where to place her advertising dollars, how best to launch a new book into the headwind of the nonstop news cycle, and every other function that bears on the publishing of her book.

The self-publisher who is serious about making the transition to profitability will usually use freelance contractors to accomplish these myriad goals. She will hire a professional editor, a book designer, and a public relations or marketing professional. She will contract for the proofing and printing of her book, and will run her own book review campaign and author tour. She will recreate the infrastructure of a publishing company, but devote it all to one book.

Recommendation: *For niche nonfiction authors, authors with a strong existing "platform" from which to sell books directly to buyers, and for those who are energized by the prospect of marketing themselves and their ideas 24/7, self-publishing can be a rewarding path.*

So, Who Are You?

I think it should be obvious by now that these paths diverge widely, although each will lead to publication of a kind. What's really critical here is your own self-examination. Why did you write your book? Who did you hope would read it? How central to your life is this book likely to be? What would you define as success with your book?

It's only by answering these questions, either alone or in consultation with a book publishing professional, that you can come to a rational decision about which path is right for you.

Five Good Reasons to Self-Publish Your Book

Amid all the discussion about self-publishing we can forget that each decision to publish is a specific, unique, and very personal calculation.

There are as many reasons to publish a book as there are people to publish them, but some authors are ideally placed to make use of the self-publishing tools available these days. You might be one of these authors if…

You are an authority in a niche field—Some authors are well known in a field that is small and easily reached through affinity magazines, on-line forums, or professional circles. With access to the likeliest market for your book and existing authority, self-publishing might be the most profitable avenue for continued sales to this type of audience.

You are a consultant to business or government—Many worthwhile books on subjects of narrow interest are published by business consultants both as a way to make money and as a way to supercharge their reputation within their field.

You are an established author trying to break into a new genre—Authors who have been pigeonholed as "nonfiction writers" or "how-to writers" can face an uphill struggle to sell any other type of book to editors. Some authors have self-published, using their existing publishing platform to establish sales, and therefore interest, for their new genre.

You are an activist with a passion for a cause—Activist authors usually have two assets that make them great candidates for self-publishing: an organization to promote their cause, and the passion that makes them spokesmen for that cause. The support of an organization, or just the assured sales to legions of followers make the economics of the publishing decision easy to calculate.

You are a novelist, short-story writer, or a poet—The vast majority of these authors will never receive a contract for a book in their lifetime. Self-publishing allows an author to see their work in print in a way they can share it with the world, which is the driving force for many writers. Many of these authors have flocked to so-called self-publishing companies on the web to realize their dreams.

When I made the decision in 1986 to publish *Body Types* it was for many of these same reasons that I've written about here: I had some expertise and a good deal of authority in this very niche subject, which was known to only a few thousand people, all of whom I knew. What's more, there were no books on the subject in print, and nothing had been written at all on the subject for many years.

In promoting *Body Types* I became an authority on a new branch of study, no matter how miniscule. The book established a place in the market, it was reordered year after year. If you're in one of the situations described here, you are well-positioned to publish your own book.

What Hasn't Changed in Self-Publishing

When Jill and I first got into self-publishing the book world was a vastly different place than it is today.

There was no Google, no Amazon, no print on demand, no blogs. There were two giant wholesalers, Baker and Taylor, and Ingram. (Well, not everything has changed.) But Ronald Reagan was president, gas cost about 90 cents a gallon, and "Magnum, P.I." was the top show on television.

Back then self-publishing was much more involved and expensive. You had to figure out how to publish a book, usually something only big companies did. You had to print at least a couple of thousand copies at a cost of several thousand dollars. These were barriers most people just couldn't get over. You had to be dedicated, driven, or desperate.

Barriers Have Shrunk

Today there are numerous websites offering publishing "packages" where all the work has been done for you (or so they claim) and by just uploading a file you can instantly become a published author.

In some cases, you can achieve this distinction without spending a penny, as long as you are willing to buy the books that result from this process. And this system has allowed many people to get into the hobby end of book publishing, which is admirable.

But self-publishing *for profit*, self-publishing as a business decision, or as an extension of a business agenda—like enhancing a consultant's reputation in her field—still requires a big dose of learning and a lot of persistence.

What Hasn't Changed

Here are some of the things that haven't changed a bit from the time of $100 cover proofs, bluelines that smelled like ammonia, and Ronald Reagan, the movie star president:

You need a rationale to publish your book—I followed Dan Poynter's outline for publishing because it fit my situation pretty well. I had the first book to be published on my subject, and an audience of several thousand people anxious to get the book. This was my rationale. I knew I would be able to pre-sell enough copies to pay the printing bill, so there was no financial risk on my part. In essence, the people who would buy those first copies made it possible to launch the book into the book trade.

 The fact that print on demand has eliminated the need for up-front sales hasn't at the same time eliminated the need for the book to have a rationale. The self-publisher still has to answer the questions of why the book needs to be published, and who will buy it.

You need to produce a high-quality book to have a chance in the market—Luckily I had worked in the publishing industry and was operating a graphic design business when I became a self-publisher. I knew how to hire an editor, and had the ability to produce a book with the same vendors who were serving the big publishers. I knew my book would be the equal to the books from my competitors, no matter who they were.

Today it's still incumbent on the self-publisher to hire editors, book designers, indexers, cover designers, and so on to get a book produced at a professional level, or to make use of a book producer who will handle the whole pre-press production of your book for you. Whichever way you go, without a commitment to quality, your book will suffer in comparison to others.

You need to be willing—no, eager—to market your book, your program, or your ideas—We launched *Body Types* with the full pre-publication review program, news releases, sample reviews, book photos, author bios, mailings with blow-back postcards, bigger publication-date review mailings, interviews and workshops. Let's face it, it's a lot of work to take on. It only makes sense if you can define your message, who it will benefit, and locate the people likely to be interested.

Today you need to answer all the same questions we had then, but now in the context of the blogosphere, social media, and the revolution that seems to be slowly unfolding in book distribution and the move to both ecommerce and epublication. The challenges of lauching and marketing a book today demand the same kind of focus, attention to the marketplace, and innovative thinking they always have.

The More Things Change...

Self-publishing remains a viable business for people in the right situation and with the right temperment. And some people are just desperate to communicate their unique vision, expression, or thoughts to the world and want to do so in a way that earns the respect of the marketplace. But almost by definition, a self-publisher is launching a business and will do themselves a favor by approaching it with the seriousness and dedication it deserves.

Another thing that hasn't changed is how powerful it is to publish a book. After spending the better part of a year writing and revising my book through lonely hours at my desk on weekends and evenings, I was able to hold the book in my hand. Now, over twenty years later I'm amazed at how long a book that provides information and usefulness to readers can last. *Body Types* has a new cover and has gone back to press for its fifth printing.

When you're ready to publish your book, do it properly because twenty years from now you may be very glad you did.

Five Things That Shouldn't Surprise You About Self-Publishing

Sometimes it's good to just kick back, push off the deadlines, turn off the ringer on the phone, and daydream a little. If you're self-employed, doesn't that mean you get to goof off once in a while? Doesn't it mean that you're the boss, not that pesky little nagging voice in your head?

Starting off in self-publishing can seem like a perilous journey. Getting into a new venture is always exciting and scary at the same time. Exciting to be doing something new, but scary because you don't necessarily know what to do first, or how to sound like you know what you're doing. But you pick it up soon enough.

As you move forward you have to keep your bearings. That means you remember what your destination was when you set out from shore, and you keep aiming for that destination until you get there.

Making Lists

Here are 5 things that shouldn't surprise you about self-publishing. They are realizations you have after you've decided to publish a book.

1. *Self-publishing is not a get-rich-quick scheme.* And I think that's been proven quite a few times by now. Yet new self-publishers have that gleam in the eye. They've read the stories, they've been to Lulu.com. Why not them?

But I'm willing to bet you didn't start writing to make a killing on the internet. You had something else in mind. Remember that thing, it will guide you well.

2. *You will meet many wonderful—and a few not so wonderful—people in indie publishing.* Truly one of the great things about social media is that it's so social. I've always been impressed by the collegiality of publishing. Maybe it's because few books compete directly with each other, but people in publishing—particularly indie publishing—are extraordinarily helpful to newcomers. And a bonus: they're pretty literate, too!

3. *You cannot imagine the variety of niches into which people are publishing.* I mean, just wander around Amazon for a while and take in the richness of interests displayed there. Here, for example, are five titles plucked almost randomly from amongst the millions of pages on Amazon:

   - *The Art of Making Fermented Sausages*
   - *Unsigned Beauties Of Costume Jewelry*
   - *Antique Sewing Tools and Tales*
   - *Exploring the World of Lucid Dreaming*
   - *The Yugo: The Rise and Fall of the Worst Car in History*

   Whatever you're interested in, there's probably some other people interested too. You just have to find them.

4. *Nonfiction publishing almost always pays—over time.* If you really do your homework, publish a book with genuine value and do just an adequate job of pushing it into the world, if you keep at it long enough, you will eventually be profitable. Of course, you have to publish

efficiently to start with, but as long as you do something to let people know your book is there, and that it can address a real need, often it's just a matter of time before someone finds it. Too many people quit trying when they haven't sold out in a few months. See #1 above.

5. *The single most important thing is to 'Be the Market.'* This is the clearest path to success for nonfiction self-publishers. If you are part of the market that's interested in the subject you've written about, you're at an advantage. You know what people need, you know the questions they're asking, and you know what was confusing when you first got into this field. That all adds up to a book with value, if you can translate your experience into teaching that helps people new to your field, or new to your level of expertise.

None of these things may surprise you, but they bear repeating, and remembering, too.

Eight Answers That Help Self-Publishers Get Up and Running

When an author decides to publish their own book they bring with them a lifetime of experience. Their books usually grow out of this experience, and capitalize on their skills and knowledge. At a minimum, you need to know *something* to write a book.

However, their experience usually doesn't include any expertise in:

- Editing, proofreading, or indexing books
- Book design, cover design, or marketing
- Book wholesaling, distribution, discounts or fulfillment
- The price of Jiffy bags or what "media mail" means

And after all, why should they know this stuff? They've been busy doing other things.

We've been surrounded by books from infancy, and pretty much take them for granted. Until it comes time to make one of our own that is, and that's when the questions begin to appear.

Let The Questions Begin!

Most beginning self-publishers have about the same questions. This allows those of us who try to help self-publishers anticipate a lot of their concerns, particularly that feeling of floating, alone, in the middle of a big sea of confusion.

Without further ado, let's look at the top questions new self-publishers have when they decide to self-publish a book:

1. *What do I do first?*

    You have to start somewhere, and the problem is you might not know exactly where that is. But the most important task you face at the beginning of your self-publishing career is to answer these two questions: "What is my goal in publishing this book? And how will I know whether or not I've been a success?" You are the only person who can answer these questions, and how you go about producing and marketing your book will depend on how you answer them. Give yourself plenty of time, and write your responses down.

2. *Do I have to start a company?*

    Okay, now you know why you answered question number one above. If your goal is to create a book for friends and family, for gifts, for fundraising or as an internal company production, you do not need to start a company to meet your goal. On the other hand, if you want to reach the widest readership possible, or make money from your book, or advocate on a large scale for a specific agenda, you are going into business, and you will need to set up a company in order to do so. Get advice from your accountant before you go any farther about how best to establish your company.

3. *Do I really need an editor?*

    See how important that first question was? If you're publishing your recipe collection, or your great aunt's recollections of her childhood, you probably don't need an editor. If you plan to get reviews, space on bookstore shelves, or speaking engagements, think about this: The biggest complaint about self-published books is *lack of editing*. You simply have to be able to pass this threshold, and freelance editors are more accessible than ever before.

4. *Do I really need an ISBN?*

If you've already decided to go for bookstore or online sales, you'll need an ISBN. If you buy your own ISBN from RR Bowker or one of their authorized vendors, you will have more flexibility and more control over the fate of your book, and your company will be listed as the publisher in book industry databases. If you use a publishing services company you may be able to save money by using their ISBN to identify your book, but they will be the publisher of record.

5. *How much is this going to cost?*

Well, that depends. There is no accurate way to answer this question (unless you consider "between nothing and $50,000" to be an answer) without more information about your book and your goals. But a lack of cash shouldn't stop you from getting into print, because there are more ways to publish than ever before. If you're planning a commercial publication, you'll need to find a book designer or book shepherd who can help you construct a budget that's appropriate for your project.

6. *It's going to take how long?*

A professionally produced book may employ editors, designers, proofreaders, illustrators, indexers and a lot of time and energy to put together properly. Selecting, hiring, coordinating all these tasks in itself takes time, not to mention the marketing chores, bibliographic listings, preparation of media kits and review copies, and allowing time for reviewers and bookings all take time. You've invested a lot in your book, now it's time to make sure you get the most out of it.

7. *Can you get my book into _____?*

Success for some authors is a review in the New York *Times*, an interview on Charlie Rose, or hitting the bestseller lists. And hey, it could happen. But if it does, it will be the result of all the work you put into the book itself and the efforts you make to spread your message as widely as possible. Nobody can guarantee that for you. Rather than a goal, think of these accomplishments as results of your work.

8. *What do you mean, discount?*

You want to see your book on Amazon.com, you think it would look great on the "New Nonfiction" table at Barnes & Noble, and you think the local independent bookstore will give you the chance for a reading. Remember that book retailers, distributors, wholesalers and book clubs are also businesses that expect to turn a profit. They are collaborators in your efforts to sell your book, and you will have to pay them for the privilege. This fact will dictate how you go about setting your retail price, so you need to learn how this part of the book business works.

The Road Forward

As you can see from the answers, there is a lot to learn when you leap into book publishing. Getting rid of the initial confusion that seems to affect most people is the fastest way to get traction for your project and take the actions that will help realize your goals.

What Does It Take to Make a Publishing Company?

Recently on PublishingPerspectives.com, the useful news and discussion site, editor-in-chief Edward Nawotka asked the question, "When does a self-publisher constitute a publishing company?"

At first you might be surprised someone would ask this question. I mean, what exactly is the point? Is there a debate going on about requirements to call yourself a publishing company?

Here's what the article says:

> So many self-publishers brand themselves as companies—for a variety of reasons, often to do with marketing—but if they just publish books written by themselves, does this qualify? Personally, I believe that it takes a list comprising three authors to have the foundation of a publishing company.

I believe Mr. Nawotka was trying to be provocative for the sake of discussion. How else to explain, for example, Para Publishing? Is it a publishing company? Not for most of its life, according to Mr. Nawotka's definition, because it only published the books of one author: Dan Poynter. Over 100 books, in fact, with sales throughout the book distribution system, for over 25 years. Seems like a publishing company, doesn't it?

Or John T. Reed, with over 30 books and selling since the 1970s. Reed had national distribution through Publishers Group West for over 20 years, although he now sells exclusively on his website. His publishing company has been highly successful for many years. Not a publishing company?

The Indie Spirit Comes to Publishing

Publishing Perspectives, which has great topical writing of interest to anyone involved with books, is also staffed by veterans of the traditional publishing industry. The prejudice against self-publishers will die hard when it finally does die.

The plain fact is that indie authors setting up publishing companies to produce and promote their own works, or the works of a small handful of authors, are here to stay. The industry is undergoing fundamental change, and the tools of production are now in everyone's hands.

How we use these tools is something different. But self-publishers are already through the gates and setting up shop and building their platforms and attracting a tribe of avid readers and selling books. Lots of books.

No, this toothpaste isn't going back into the tube. Indie authors don't really need someone telling them whether they can be considered a "publishing company" or not—it's an irrelevant question.

There's no licensing authority where you get a permit to publish a book, or where you go to get permission to call yourself a publishing company. The new model is authors talking directly to readers, without a big corporate publisher in between.

This is a model that's exciting to a lot of readers and to a lot of writers too. Big trade publishers, on the other hand, have always been business-to-business companies, suppliers of products to distributors and wholesalers with very little contact with the end users of their products—actual book buyers.

And that's why indie authors continue to succeed: we are the market we are selling to. And that counts a lot more than what you call yourself, don't you think?

Is It Time to Kill "Jerry"?

In 2000, screenwriter John Blumenthal self-published his comic novel, *What's Wrong With Dorfman?* after his manuscript had been rejected 75 times. (You know, I have to admire a writer who believes in their book that much. I'm not sure how anxious I would be to resubmit my book after 30, 40, or 50 rejections.)

In any event, people kept telling Blumenthal how much they loved the book, even though they were rejecting it for publication. So he decided to take matters into his own hands, set up a publishing company, and self-published his book.

A Self-Publishing Success

Dorfman was selected by *January* magazine as one of the 50 best books of the year. Blumenthal went on to get other major reviews and eventually sold the book to St. Martin's Press.

Blumenthal has also published with Simon & Schuster and Ballentine. He sold over 4,000 copies of his self-published *What's Wrong With Dorfman?* by working relentlessly at promotion. But he realized his company, Farmer Street Press, would need someone to play the role of publisher. That's how "Jerry" was born.

As he said in BooksnBytes.com:

There was no Jerry. Jerry was me. Every self-publisher should have a Jerry, although you can call him Bob or Moishe or Deepak, it's up to you. Jerry was the front man. He put his name on press releases etc. I wanted people to think Farmer Street Press was a real company. Unfortunately, I had to fire Jerry because we just didn't see eye to eye on a lot of things.

"Jerry" Has Plenty of Ancestors

Before so many people jumped into self-publishing, we tried mightily to disguise what we were doing. Somehow a publishing company run by John Smith (for example), publishing a book by John Smith, publicized by a PR person named John Smith does not, perhaps, convey the best message to those you are trying to sell to. Or at least that's what we thought.

One of my publishing mentors, Felix Morrow, created the Mystic Arts Book Society, an early negative-option book club. He had to have a monthly magazine in which the editor picked the books for the month and wrote them up for the membership.

Felix realized that among the many new books he would be promoting through his book club, there would be some he couldn't sell himself. Felix had a long history as a writer and publisher and some of the subjects Mystic Arts dealt in were considered to be "fringe" or "alternative" or "counterculture" at the time.

His solution: he created an editor for his book club, John Wilson, who was really Felix's alter ego. As John Wilson he could find books for his members and had complete freedom to write the copy he needed for his monthly newsletter.

As Felix would say, when we talked about the possibility of duplicating his book club in the 1990s, "I needed John Wilson. He could say things that Felix Morrow could never say!"

Time to Kill Them Off?

We've entered a whole new world when it comes to self-publishing and independent publishing. Like musicians a few years ago, it's now seen as useful, almost obligatory, for authors to have direct contact with their readers, and we are constantly being bombarded by advice to build our author platform and dialogue with readers to establish a community of interest around the books we write and publish.

In this new model, it's authenticity that counts. We have authors blogging about their creative process, about their editorial progress, about how much money they are making from the sales of their books.

On Twitter we can follow our favorite authors and interact with them in ways we never could have imagined a few years ago.

With this wave of contact, communication and authenticity, do we really need the "Jerrys" and the "John Wilsons" of the past? Authors now establish publishing companies, hire editors, designers and book printers, and proudly declare themselves author/businesspeople in the marketplace.

It could be time to kill these guys off. What do you think? Do we still need to keep up the artifice, to pretend we are really a small publisher, not a guy in the dining room with a laptop? Would it matter any more?

How to Get Unstuck

Publishing a book can take quite a bit of time. Sometimes you finish a manuscript after months or years of work, and you feel like you're ready to go.

But then you realize you need to hire an editor, and it's back to "hurry up and wait" while another editorial process takes place.

Or your book might be done, but you're not sure what to do next, so you spend all your time researching. You've got 120 blogs on your feed reader, you know the names of all the print on demand companies, but you have no book.

And then sometimes you've already finished the manuscript, printed your book, and now you realize you need a plan—or something—to know what to do next.

Never fear, there are always a few ways to get off the dime and back on track.

So no matter where you are in the process, here are some ideas to help out.

9 Things You Can Do Right Now to Get Unstuck

If you haven't finished your book:

1. Get some other opinions, circulate parts of the manuscript to friends or sympathetic readers. Whether you agree with their assessment or not, you'll have a new perspective on your material.

2. Think about hiring an editor to help put your manuscript in order. Editors can be incredibly skillful at helping authors shape their manuscripts. More experienced authors know this and use editors to help their process.

3. Visit writer forums for referrals, advice, a community of others in the same situation. Hey, you're online anyway, join a couple of active writer's forums and you'll find a sympathetic community of other writers.

If your manuscript's done, but you're not sure what to do next:

4. Sit down and decide how to self-publish to meet your goals. Will it be private, just circulated to friends and family, or for a fundraiser? On sale? Or will you try to compete actively in the marketplace? Each path has its own requirements, and that will help orient you.

5. Look into hiring a publishing consultant, a book shepherd or a book designer to help you establish schedules, budgets and priorities. Use their experience to move you to the next step.

6. Go back and make sure you have the infrastructure in place to establish your publishing enterprise. Have you acquired your ISBNs? Filled out directory listings for your publishing company? These details can be overlooked in the beginning.

If your book's been published, now what?

7. If you haven't done so, register the domain of your book's name. Get a blog attached to the domain and start writing about the topic of your book. Don't try

to sell the book, just work on finding an audience with common interests.

8. Go over and set up a Facebook fan page for your book. It only takes a few minutes, and you can let all your friends and followers know about it right away.

9. If you know other people with websites or blogs in your field, offer to write free articles for them. It will introduce you to groups of new readers every time.

There's No Substitute for a Plan

All of these suggestions will get you moving again, and that's a good thing. But what self-publishers really need in order to stay on track is a realistic and orderly plan. Your plan should include all three of these phases of publication; finishing your manuscript, planning for publication, and long-term marketing.

With a plan in hand, you know where you are, and you know where you have to go. Without a plan it's just too easy to get bogged down in detail and lose sight of the larger picture.

Book publishing can require lots of decisions and lots of different actions over a period of months. Be a smart publisher: get your plan together first.

Top 10 Worst Self-Publishing Mistakes—Explained!

I love those "Top 10" lists David Letterman uses on his show, and the way they count up from 10 to 1. One day I thought, "Why can't we have something like that?"

Talking to authors and new self-publishers, you hear a lot of misconceptions, errors of fact and other mistakes simply because people are new to the field.

To help cure the world of these mistakes, here's my own take on a Top 10 List for self-publishers of mistakes to avoid. I hope you enjoy it.

10. You thought you could re-use that ISBN you paid so much for since the novel you put it on last year isn't selling anyway.
Explained: You never want to re-use an ISBN, or even use it for another edition of the same book. The ISBN is known as a unique identifier. It's intended to be assigned to one edition of one book. You book's information has been entered in book databases everywhere, and you will only create tremendous confusion between the two works, hurting sales for both, if you attempt to re-use an ISBN. Just don't do it.

9. Everybody knows the words to the song, so it's okay to quote lyrics from it throughout your novel, right?
Explained: I read a blog post recently about using bits of songs in your writing. The author found, after using only snippets of 1960s songs in a party scene, that he had a liabil-

ity of over $6,000. Just like paintings, poems, or any creative expression, people's lyrics and music are protected by copyright law, and violations of this law can be expensive and very damaging. If you want to use it, get permission first.

8. The photos looked fine on your screen, and that means they will look fine when they're printed, it just makes sense.
Explained: Graphics on screens are all displayed at a resolution of 72 dots per inch (dpi) in Reg-Green-Blue (RGB) colorspace. That's just the way computers display graphics. However, when you go to print your book, your color photos will need to be 300 dpi in the Cyan-Magenta-Yellow-Black (CMYK) colorspace. So no, the image you see on your screen, no matter how gorgeous, may not have enough resolution to print well.

7. I picked Arial for my book because the name reminded me of my middle school girlfriend.
Explained: Many people don't notice typefaces, typography, design, serifs, ligatures, and other elements book designers take for granted, and why should they? But that doesn't mean it doesn't matter what typeface you use. The classic book typefaces, when used correctly, will produce a book that's beautiful, readable, and reader-friendly. That's why they're classics.

6. I know they're charging me $6,000 to publish my book, but I get 10 copies, absolutely free!
Explained: Well, $6,000 divided by 10 is … The point here is that if you want to publish your own book you may be better off using a plain author services company like CreateSpace or Lulu than a subsidy publisher. Why? The subsidy pub-

lisher makes its money from sales to authors—that's you. If you use a service like CreateSpace you are the publisher and you use them as a printer. You pay only for the services you decide you need, and then you make your money from book sales.

5. I thought it would sound more impressive if I wrote my memoir in the third person. All my sports heroes talk that way.

Explained: By far the best way for most authors to present their information in nonfiction books is with a clear, active, straightforward style. Attempts to create unusual styles, strange viewpoints, exotic points of view almost always fail since they are incredibly difficult to carry off well. Both you and your readers will be well served by a natural conversational style that follows a normal and expected narrative. This will make your valuable information stand out, and readers won't be distracted by an eccentric writing style.

4. I really got the unit price down, but I had to print 10,000 copies. You have any room in your garage?

Explained: Having a plan on how you intend to market, publicize and sell your book before entering into book production is highly recommended. The unit cost of your book is meaningless if you never sell any. Many self-publishers are using digital printing through print on demand distribution to minimize this type of risk. However, you have to plan your book, its retail price, and your method of distribution before going to press.

3. Sure, I included an invoice with all the books I sent to book reviewers. Hey, they don't care, it's just a big company paying the bill.

Explained: Although reviewers do usually work for larger companies, sending an invoice with a review copy will ensure that you won't get paid for the book, and you won't get a review either. The convention is that you are asking for valuable editorial time and space in a publication, and certainly the least you can expect is to provide a book to anyone gracious enough to go to the trouble of reviewing your book.

   2. It was cheaper to print my novel as an 8-1/2" x 11" book because I got so many words on each page.
Explained: Although it's true that you can save money in digital printing by creating a book with fewer pages, a novel printed full page on letter-size paper with small margins and tight lines to get a lot of words on a page is likely to be read by no one. Making your book difficult to read is a quick way to eliminate readers. There is no economy in printing books that no one wants to read.

   1. What do you mean, I need a cover designer? Don't books come with covers?
Explained: Most author services companies are only too happy to put a cover on your book for a fee, or to turn you loose on their cover creation programs. But it's pretty easy to tell which books that have been produced this way, and it isn't a pretty picture. If your book is worth publishing, and you want people to buy it, and you understand the cover is the primary way that people will identify the book wherever it appears, don't you think it might be worthwhile to get a cover designer you can afford to create a cover for you?

That's my list, you might have your own. If there was any doubt, you now know some good things to avoid when it comes time to publish your book.

The Secret to Successful Self-Publishing

The effort involved in self-publishing is never trivial. But there's a chance that, in the end, you might discover the secret to successful self-publishing. That's what happened to me, and I'm going to tell you how I discovered it.

The Journey to this Point

Of course, even to get to the point of having a book ready to go to press, you may have:

- started a publishing company,
- opened bank accounts, merchant accounts, Paypal accounts, and created an identity for your company,
- registered your company with RR Bowker and the *Books in Print* database, to get your ISBNs,
- figured out how the book distribution system works, or might work for your company,
- established a presence on the internet and in social media to promote the launch of your book,
- found freelance service providers for editorial, design and production help, or if not,
- worked out how to edit, layout, proofread and paginate your book, then make a PDF for your printer,

In short, you've done whatever was necessary to create the infrastructure of a company and make sure your book is available to buyers as best you can.

It Was Fun While it Lasted

I followed this same path when I became a self-publisher. Just the power of bringing a brand new book into existence was intoxicating. It felt like I had a power I had never imagined I could exercise. It was awesome.

Putting a book together is a creative and exciting activity. Picking covers, typefaces, categories, and trying to position the book in its genre exercise some fine faculties. But when it comes to marketing and sales, for all too many people it becomes a long, hard road. Most successful self-published books take quite a while to become a success.

Oh, sure, there's always someone you read about who got a contract from a big publisher, or sold the rights to a movie producer. But I'd wager the majority of self-published books are abandoned by their authors. It's just too hard to keep swimming against the stream.

Here's something I read last month by agent Chip Mac-Gregor, in response to a question:

> Publishers bascially sell in lines—that is, if they are currently selling a lot of fitness and health titles, they're going to want to publish more fitness and health titles in the future, since they know how to market and sell those. … "THIS book is similar to THAT book. If you could get excited about THAT title, you're sure to like THIS title." Make sense?

The Secret Is Out

It dawned on me one day that I had done all this work to establish my publishing company and all the connections it needed to exist within the publishing industry, and all my chances for success were riding on one book. Every time I sold a book, I hoped to have a happy customer, but I wasn't kidding myself. I knew they weren't going to buy two copies of the book.

I realized that I now had the machinery in place to actually become a *publisher*. In my case, not just a self-publisher, but a publisher of other people's work as well. And why not? With a contract, I could relive the fun of making books and, when the book was finished, I now had two products to sell that same customer.

In short, I went from being an author to being a businessman.

And this is the secret to success in self-publishing:

Start thinking about your next book today. Right now.

Take Chip MacGregor's advice. Look at your book, and see which direction you could extend what you've started. Here are some ideas:

- If your book presented a theory of something, you might create a *workbook* to complement it.
- If you wrote a history, think about a biography of the most important figure of that era.
- If you created a self-help book to address the needs of a specific population, what other challenges is that population likely to face?

- For a follow up to a business book, think about creating a book of case studies.
- To follow up on a book concerning social issues, create a sequel that tells how the story has continued to develop. Were you right?
- Novelists write sequels, prequels, stories in the same era, or simply in the same genre.

And I'm sure you can think of many more of your own.

In other words, put yourself inside the brain and heart of your reader, the reader who has just finished your book with satisfaction. How can you help further the understanding you've already started?

We Live in a World of Complex Interconnectedness

Every discipline connects to the world at numerous points, each of which are fertile ground for further work. John McPhee, the great American essayist and writer, started writing a magazine article about oranges. Just regular, Florida oranges, nothing fancy. Before he had finished, he had written a whole book about oranges. Every part of orange farming touched many other activities, other markets, science, meteorology, the history of the orange industry and the personalities who shaped it.

Each facet of the problem that you study and write about, that you explain to your readers, constructs a bigger, and more complete picture of your study to your tribe.

Once you have two books, or three, or a whole series of books on your specialty, you gain authority and influence in your field. The cost of every promotion you do is spread across all your titles, giving you that much more chance to succeed.

You have many pillars to help support your publishing enterprise. By diversifying, you have also spread your risk. You learn from early missteps, and become more efficient, savvier with each book. You learn to listen to your market, to find solutions to their problems, satisfaction for their needs.

Congratulations. You are on your way to success in self-publishing.

Things I Love—and Hate—About Self-Publishing

Did you ever feel like you lived on both sides of a border, an issue, a trend?

I love self-publishing because of the absolute finality of the process. At the end, you are left with a book in your hand, one that will probably outlast you and most of the people you know. There aren't many occupations where you get to leave such a tangible mark, where you can hold the results of your hard work and your investment of time, money and attention.

But . . . when I cruise writer's websites I'm reminded of just how much I dislike the prejudice that persists in many parts of the publishing world against authors who decide to publish their own books. Despite the explosive growth of self-publishing, the invasion of a tradition-bound industry by the indie spirit, many writers continue to heap scorn on self-published authors. Even more infuriating is the obvious ignorance about self-publishing that these writers exhibit in their comments.

I love the creative expression that self-publishing provides to the entrepreneurial author. It's an old truism that the power of the press belongs to the person who owns the press. Modern self-publishing has taken this idea to an extreme. Now, you only have to own a computer with an internet connection to own the printing press. A writer who wants to share her work with others, or to profit by selling directly to interested readers, has a significant amount of influence that was unavailable before.

But . . . many writers have used this power to publish unreadable, unresearched, and uninteresting books that nobody will read, let alone buy. For many of these books, this didn't have to happen. Like everyone else, authors can be lazy, prejudiced, inept, or close-minded, and self-publishing brings more of these books into existence.

I love how when you self-publish you get to decide what your book is called, what it will cost, what it will look like, when it will be published, and how you will sell it. Do you want a book with a completely black cover, 5" x 8" and with 700 pages? Hey, why not? There's nobody to tell you not to do it, and the expense involved can be held to such a low level that there's no reason not to experiment with what you think might be of interest to your readers. I love that the freedom to make these decisions is in the hands of authors.

But . . . it amazes me that fear and elitism continue to rule many writers' ideas about publication. I can't tell you how often, reading a writer's blog or a discussion of publishing, that I've come across this sentiment: "Well, if I keep getting rejected, it means I'm not ready for publication. Agents and editors are the best judges of what should and shouldn't be published and, if I never get an acceptance, I'll just accept that my work was never good enough, and that's okay with me." And every time, it leaves me heartbroken.

How did we learn to hand so much power over our creative life to someone else? This kind of respectful timidity has condemned many writers to a life of frustration. I want to grab them by the shoulders, give them a big shake, and tell them, "Wake up! It's not the 19th century any more. Publish your book and let the dictators be damned. If you sell a bunch of copies, they will line up at your door. You are the creative one, you are the content creator, the idea generator. Don't give up your autonomy so quickly!"

I love when there's a close collaboration between an author and the publishing professionals they bring in to help get their book to market. Skilled editors, designers, printers and marketers in the service of a clear concept and a sound marketing strategy can produce truly unusual and valuable books that might never have seen the light of day from a traditional publisher. I love being involved in these projects, where the author has determined to put out a book that competes with the best books coming from big publishers.

But . . . it's still true that self-publishers can't match the distribution power of a traditional publishing house, and the entire book distribution system is geared toward only the books of big publishers and well-established niche publishers with a line of books. I hate the way the distribution system works—and I'm not alone on this—to make the bookstores of America into a vast consignment operation, where your book, if it doesn't sell in a few weeks, is likely to get returned to your warehouse (or your garage) with barely time for the ink to dry.

The "blockbuster" mentality can only work for big companies with deep pockets who are willing to make big bets. The careful, community-nurturing, personal type of publishing that works for self-publishers has virtually no home in the book distribution system, and that's a shame.

I love the digital printing revolution and the print on demand distribution model that have produced such big benefits for self-publishers. This technology has allowed thousands of people to publish a book with almost no financial risk, and without the depressing sight of their garage filled with unsold books in aging cardboard cartons.

Print on demand has done more for self-publishing than any other innovation to date, and I love the ability to quickly and economically issue a book. We can respond quickly to events in our niche, or simply experiment with content focus, size, cover graphics and other parts of the product cycle because the risk and financial exposure of printing books has been almost eliminated.

But . . . when authors go looking for a way to get their book into print, all too often they are seduced by misleading or downright fraudulent advertising by the industry that's sprung up to sell services to these authors. So-called self-publishing companies sell inflated packages of services of unknown quality to unsuspecting authors who are confused about the process of publishing or unwilling to take the time to educate themselves about the difference between a book printer and a subsidy publisher.

Although there are reputable and enthusiastic subsidy houses if you look for them, the biggest operators seem to capture all the advertising space and media attention, leading even more authors into the clutches of what may well become an expensive, restrictive and frustrating publishing situation that can be hard to disengage from.

I love the ability to take ideas you've been thinking about for many years and translate them into a medium that can be read and appreciated by any interested person. I love the power it gives to thinkers and writers to spread their concepts and solutions to problems. Without having to survive the rigors of querying agents, or the year or two of waiting until your book comes out, you can take an edited and prepared manuscript to print in a matter of weeks.

But . . . many of the authors who've decided to "let someone else do it" and ended up at one of the less palatable subsidy publishers often have reason to regret their decision in the first place. An authr who has paid for substandard editing, lackluster book design and book prices that doomed their book as unsaleable may well come to the conclusion that they never should have started at all, and that's a shame.

Even the self-publishers who want to migrate to a better supplier have a hard time escaping the subsidy publisher when they find out they cannot get their cover artwork, even if they paid for it. Or if they request a PDF of the book interior to use elsewhere, they might find their subsidy publisher will only supply them with a "watermarked" version that will need substantial work before it can be used for book production. That's just mean, and I hate it when it happens to unsuspecting authors whose only crime was to skip a bit of homework, or who got taken in by hyped-up marketing.

What About You?

Having been a self-published author, a publisher of other authors' books and a book producer designing and helping authors bring their books to market, I've seen the best outcomes, and some of the worst. There's a lot to love about self-publishing, and a lot to hate. My hope is that by educating yourself, you'll avoid the worst of these situations and end up with a book you can be proud of, and which you can sell for a profit. I love that idea.

26 Ways to Win at Self-Publishing

I visit a lot of blogs about publishing, writing and related topics. There's a huge interest in self-publishing, and it seems that many developments in the publishing world are helping to stimulate that interest. New technologies, new devices, new formats are making it easier and easier for authors to get their work out into the world by making an end run around the gates that the gatekeepers are so fervently guarding.

Balancing the interest and opportunities is the drumbeat of warnings, prejudice and downright threats that seek to discourage people from diving into the independent publishing pool. "You'll ruin your career." "My friend spent $10,000 and all he has is a garage full of books." "We'll be buried in an avalanche of crappy books."

It seems pointless sometimes to engage with these attitudes, since there often seems to be a fixed idea behind them: self-publishing is for losers, people who couldn't get published any other way. And nothing you can say will change this view. It's my opinion that this attitude arises from some need for personal validation, but hey, that's just me.

This Is For The Winners

Many people "win" at self-publishing. That's because there are lots of reasons why authors decide to publish their own books. Some self-published books aren't even meant for sale, and will never change hands for money. Some are published for reasons that have nothing to do with monetary reward, career advancement, or ego gratification.

People are funny. Given the chance, tens of thousands of ordinary people have decided to publish their own books over the last few years, and more are certainly on the way. I applaud every one of these authors for taking their destiny into their own hands, for turning a deaf ear to the people who said "You can't do it," or "You'll look a fool." They accomplished something. They expressed themselves in the world—these are not small things.

So I've put together this list of ways that you can "win" at self-publishing. In this context, "winning" can be a moment of tremendous personal satisfaction. It can be accolades from your peers. It can be the joy of accomplishment. If you're reading this, you're probably a writer. What would "winning" be for you? Here's my list:

26 Ways to Win at Self-Publishing

1. You finally get the book finished, printed and in your hand: *you win*

2. At last you have a chance to fully explain the ideas you've been thinking and talking about for years: *you win*

3. You get an interview in the local paper as a "published author": *you win*

4. You send a copy of your book to your ex mother-in-law: *you win*

5. You get interviewed by a local radio show and people actually call in to ask questions: *you win*

6. You're invited to write an article on your specialty in a trade magazine, and they actually publish it, referring to you as the author of...: *you win*

7. You create a course based on your book and sell it to the local adult education center: *you win*

8. You speak at the Lions or Elks or other fraternal club on the subject of your book: *you win*

9. The local bookstore lets you have a book launch party for your book, and everyone shows up: *you win*

10. You wander into an indie bookstore in another town, and find your book on their shelf: *you win*

11. You gift wrap a copy and hand it to your mother, watching her unwrap it: *you win*

12. You send an autographed copy to your 8th grade English teacher: *you win*

13. You take a table at a street fair and sell your book, encountering people who just want to talk about your subject: *you win*

14. You overhear coworkers talking, and one mentions that you've published a book: *you win*

15. Every one of the people you care about tell you how much they love your book: *you win*

16. You give a talk to a local writer's group about self-publishing and find yourself answering many questions: *you win*

17. Your dad pulls you aside at the next family gathering and tells you how proud he is that you dedicated the book to him: *you win*

18. Your alumni news writes you up with a picture of your book cover and some nice blurbs: *you win*

19. You send an advance copy to someone you've never met, but who you respect, and they send you a glowing endorsement to use: *you win*

20. Readers keep asking you when the next book in the series will be out, and you know they mean it: *you win*

21. You realize you've sold enough books to pay your printing bill, that all the rest are profit: *you win*

22. You receive a request from someone you don't know for permission to quote from your book: *you win*

23. You open your mail and find a check from your distributor that you didn't expect: *you win*

24. A friend at a party asks if you're still looking for an agent, and for a moment you don't understand the question: *you win*

25. Your local library buys two copies of your book: *you win*

26. You start to think about other books you've always wanted to write and can now publish: *you win*

The secret is this: when you publish your own book, you get to decide what winning looks like, how success feels. You've taken back control of your writing destiny. You know winning comes in many ways, in many small moments, and you can finally relax and savor them.

When you self-publish, you get to define success, to set goals for your own publication. In a way, you've already won.

Bookmaking

Does Book Design Really Matter?

Did you ever see the movie "Deception" that came out in 2008? No? It starred Ewan McGregor, Hugh Jackman and Michelle Williams. The cast alone should have made it a hit, but it bombed; critics hated it and audiences ignored it in spectacular numbers.

Despite Hollywood's addiction to stars and hype over content, the dirty little secret is that—Harry Potter aside—no one knows which movies will be hits and which will flop, until they open. Once actual ticket-buying people start to go to the movie, word quickly spreads about the *experience* people had, and they always tell their friends. This is what makes or breaks a movie, and everyone knows it.

No one expected "The Blair Witch Project," shot for under $100,000 to be a hit, but word of mouth sent it to a total box office over $248 million worldwide.

Movies and Books: Not That Different

The same is frequently true of books. It's the *experience* people have reading the book that makes them want to share it with friends.

And besides the content itself, the only other influence on the experience of reading a book is exercised by the book designer. There is no make up, no locations, cinematography, special effects, stereo sound systems, none of the bells and whistles that grab attention in a film.

Remarks to the G-20 Summit

Six months ago, I said that the London Summit marked a turning point in the G20's effort to prevent economic catastrophe. And here in Pittsburgh, we've taken several significant steps forward to secure our recovery, and transition to strong, sustainable, and balanced economic growth. We brought the global economy back from the brink. We laid the groundwork today for long-term prosperity, as well.

It's worth recalling the situation we faced six months ago -- a contracting economy, skyrocketing unemployment, stagnant trade, and a financial system that was nearly frozen. Some were warning of a second Great Depression. But because of the bold and coordinated action that we took, millions of jobs have been saved or created; the decline in output has been stopped; financial markets have come back to life; and we stopped the crisis from spreading further to the developing world.

Still, we know there is much further to go. Too many Americans are still out of work, and struggling to pay bills. Too many families are uncertain about what the future will bring. Because our global economy is now fundamentally interconnected, we need to act together to make sure our recovery creates new job_____
imbalances and

Pittsburgh was
known its share
could no longer
up, and it dusted
creating industri
energy. It serves
century econom
prosperity lies n
ington -- but in p

Today, we took
perity, and to fo
and Balanced G

125

REMARKS TO THE G-20 SUMMIT

Six months ago, I said that the London Summit marked a turning point in the G20's effort to prevent economic catastrophe. And here in Pittsburgh, we've taken several significant steps forward to secure our recovery, and transition to strong, sustainable, and balanced economic growth. We brought the global economy back from the brink. We laid the groundwork today for long-term prosperity, as well.

It's worth recalling the situation we faced six months ago -- a contracting economy, skyrocketing unemployment, stagnant trade, and a financial system that was nearly frozen. Some were warning of a second Great Depression. But because of the bold and coordinated action that we took, millions of jobs have been saved or created; the decline in output has been stopped; financial markets have come back to life; and we stopped the crisis from spreading further to the developing world.

Still, we know there is much further to go. Too many Americans are still out of work, and struggling to pay bills. Too many families are uncertain about what the future will bring. Because our global economy is now fundamentally interconnected, we need to act together to make sure our recovery creates new jobs and industries, while preventing the kinds of imbalances and abuse that led us into this crisis.

Pittsburgh was a perfect venue for this work. This city has known its share of hard times, as older industries like steel could no longer sustain growth. But Pittsburgh picked itself up, and it dusted itself off, and is making the transition to job-creating industries of the future—from biotechnology to clean energy. It

125

No, the work of book design is quiet, always taking a back seat to what the author has to say, or the story she is telling.

An Example

Even though it's so subtle, or so humble, as to be completely overlooked, book design can be crucial in determining the kind of experience your readers have. Let's look at the sample pages opposite.

The top image is not untypical of what you might receive from someone who has no idea what a book design is supposed to look like. The second version is more characteristic of a careful book design.

Which version would you rather read? To which one do you think reviewers or buyers will respond more positively? Which one do you think is likely to provide a better experience for the reader, and hence, more likely to be recommended to friends?

In professional publishing circles—and that includes chain bookstore buyers, book reviewers, and other people you are might solicit for blurbs, reviews, or purchases—this is common knowledge and widespread. When you are preparing to publish a book, think carefully about whether the cost of a book design is truly a cost or whether it's an investment in the book you've put so much into, and on which you may have a lot riding. You can only launch your book once—make sure it gets the attention it deserves.

And now for a round-up of opinions from around the web on the importance of interior book design:

If you want positive word-of-mouth, getting the interior right is far more important than the cover.
—*Morris Rosenthal, Self-Publishing 2.0*

Professionally edited, typeset, & designed are critical for success via POD. (Looks count.)
—*Jane Friedman, Publishing Passion, publisher and editorial director of the Writer's Digest brand community*

Unless you have professional graphic design experience, hire someone who does!
—*Dummies.com*

For most books, you may find that you are ahead of the game by paying a professional to do the layout and typesetting. Yes, it will cost you — usually in the hundreds of dollars (but could easily exceed $1,000). You will have a more professional product (that will enhance the reader's experience rather than detract from it) and will have saved yourself a lot of time and headaches.
—*Walt Shiel, Slipdown Mountain Publications, View from the Publishing Trenches blog*

After many hours in book stores and libraries, the light bulbs began to pop in my head. Oh, so that's how a beautiful cook book looks. It should not look like something produced by the church committee on a home computer—it should look like a professional publishing house produced it. Right—now the search for a graphic designer began. Wow!! I could not believe

the transformation. I sold over 250,000 copies of *Fit to Cook – Why 'Waist' Time in the Kitchen?* It's a guarantee that the book would not have sold 250 copies in its original format.
—*Denise Hamilton, Ink Tree, Ltd.*

About a quarter of the self-pubbed titles we've reviewed have gone on to be republished by big presses, but I'd have to say that all of them are of comparable quality to traditionally published books—otherwise we wouldn't waste the space on them.
—*Lyn Miller-Lachmann, Blogger and Editor,*
   Multicultural Review

Self-published doesn't mean slapdash. Don't self-publish your book until it's as good as you'd like it to be had a mainstream publisher put it out there. Self-publishing isn't a shortcut to print. It's an alternative business model for aspiring writers. You wouldn't set up a bakery and sell cakes where the icing was all over the place and the body was sunken in the middle. So don't think it's acceptable to put your book out there with a bunch of typos and a cover made from Clip Art.
—*Dan Holloway, danholloway.wordpress.com*

For me, as a reader, a writer and a designer, book design matters. And I think it should matter for all self-publishers who want to give their book the best possible chance for success.

Book Design Tips for Authors

Some books involve book designers right from their conception. These are books in which the way the content is presented is intrinsic to the purpose of the book. Think of manuals, travel books, workbooks that accompany another text or a seminar. These are all examples of books where design will play an important role right from the beginning.

General nonfiction books are less likely to involve designers at the beginning. But that doesn't mean authors shouldn't start paying attention to how their books are put together. I think it's fair to say that authors who are truly concerned about communicating their message effectively to their readers will pay attention to the design of their books.

Consistency is Important

Many design issues can wait until the manuscript is complete. The principle thing for authors to think about while writing their book is consistency. Books, by their nature, need to be consistent. Cues are sent to readers, often below their level of awareness, about how the book is organized and what to expect as they proceed through the book.

Here are some points to think about as your manuscript comes together. With all these suggestions, keep the reader uppermost in your mind. You're writing to be read. Every other consideration ought to be secondary to getting the reader your information in the best possible way for them to consume it.

Book division—Decide whether you'll divide your book into chapters. Decide if you'll use parts to organize the chapters into coherent sections, and if there's a good reason to do this. For instance, if your book covers a wide range of time, it might make sense to impose a structure by dividing the main sections of the book into different parts, then, below those, to divide content into individual chapters.

Non-text elements—Be consistent in how you number chapters, parts, tables, figures, charts, and so on. A good method for numbering graphics is to use both the chapter number plus a sequential item number. For instance, in chapter 1, the graphics (or tables or figures) might be numbered Figure 1-1, Figure 1-2, and so on. In chapter 2, start the numbering over again, like this: Figure 2-1, Figure 2-2 and so on. This will make it immediately obvious to everyone working on the book which graphics go where. It also keeps your references simpler and easier to track.

Epigraphs—(Not epitaphs, which appear on tombstones!) These are the quotations authors like to put on the chapter opening page. If you put these on one or two chapters, readers will expect to find them on every chapter. And if the first six epigraphs are one liners, do you really need that half-page quote you stuck into chapter 10? No, you don't.

Bold type—Don't use bold within the text of your book. It won't look good, it's non-standard and it devalues the text around it. If you need to emphasize something, use italics or re-write so it has a natural emphasis from the structure of your prose. Bold is fine in heads and sub-heads or for run-in heads at the beginning of list items.

Formatting—Don't kill yourself formatting. Most of the formatting authors do in their manuscripts ends up on the layout designer's floor, discarded as useless to the book construction process.

Styles—Learn to use styles instead of local formatting. Are you using Microsoft Word? Have you ever looked at the style menu or style palette? Putting in 20 minutes to learn to use styles (and it won't take longer, I promise) will save you many hours of tedium in your writing life. And you want to spend your time writing, not formatting, don't you?

Tabs—Eliminate the use of tabs within the text of your document. Tabs are unnecessary unless you're creating tables or other non-text graphics. Your designer will only have to strip them out, and any tabs inadvertently left in the file could be problematic later in the design process.

Spacing—Don't double space between sentences.

Backups—Make a backup. Make another one, and email it to yourself. This is the fastest and safest off-site backup you can get. And it won't cost you anything. The file, as an attachment to your email will sit on your email server until you decide to delete it (check your email client settings to see if messages are automatically deleted after some specific amount of time has elapsed.)

A lot of these suggestions are aimed at manuscripts you are preparing to send to a book designer or layout artist. While you're working on your book you probably will do lots of formatting because it simply makes the document easier to understand and more visually enjoyable to work with.

Work on a copy of your file instead. Designate it as a backup because you will delete it when you change the master file, then create another copy to work on. You don't want to end up with more than one version of your file, if both have unsynchronized changes.

Paying a little attention to how your book is going to look, how it will be constructed, will pay off when you go into production. Your book will get to press more quickly, it will be more consistent, and it will be better at communicating your content.

Cover Design Tips for Self-Publishers

We've all seen them. The train wrecks. The art class projects. The cringe-inducing artwork. It's the world of do-it-yourself book cover design.

Somewhere between the quirky "cover design generators" on author-service company websites, and the All-American view that everyone should get a ribbon because, after all, they participated, the cover design is suffering at the hands of self-publishers.

And no, I'm not saying that self-published books aren't getting better—there are a lot of great-looking indie books out there. But I am saying that you don't have to go far to find the ones that went wrong.

Book cover design, at its height, is truly an art form, no matter how commercial. The best book designers continue to amaze and surprise us with their graphic design prowess.

But anyone who can write and publish a book ought to be able to avoid at least the worst mistakes in cover design.

So, here without further ado, are my cover design tips for self-publishers.

Establish a principal focus for the cover—Nothing is more important. Your book is about something, and the cover ought to reflect that one idea clearly.

One element should take control, command the overwhelming majority of attention, of space, and emphasis on the cover. Don't fall into the trap of loading up your cover with too many elements, three or four photos, illustrations, maps, or floating bits of graphics.

You could think of your book cover like a billboard, trying to catch the attention of browsers as they speed by. Billboards usually have 6 words or less. You have to "get it" at 60 miles per hour, in 3 to 5 seconds.

A book cover ought to do the same thing. At a glance your prospect ought to know,

- the genre of your book,
- the general subject matter or focus, and
- some idea of the tone or ambiance of the book.

Is it a thriller? A software manual? A memoir of your time in Fiji? Your ideas on reform of the monetary system? Each of these books needs a cover that tells at a glance what the book is about.

Make everything count—If you are going to introduce a graphic element, make sure it helps you communicate with the reader.

Use the background—Avoid white backgrounds, which will disappear on the websites of online retailers, most of who use white backgrounds. Use a color, a texture, or a background illustration instead.

Make your title large—Reduce your cover design on screen to the size of a thumbnail on Amazon and see if you can read it. Can you make out what it's about? If not, simplify.

Use a font that's easy to read—See above. There's no sense using a font that's unreadable when it's radically reduced.

Particularly watch out for script typefaces, the kind that look lacy and elegant at full size. They often disappear when small.

Find images that clarify—Try not to be too literal. Look for something that expresses the mood, historical period, or overall tone of the book; provide a context.

Stay with a few colors—If you don't feel comfortable picking colors, look at some of the color palettes available online to get a selection of colors that will work well together, or take a look at books in the bookstore you find appealing and copy their color combinations.

Look at lots of great book covers—You may not be able to mimic all their techniques, but the best book covers are tremendous sources of inspiration and fresh ideas.

Taking a little care with a book cover you're designing yourself can produce big results. Look at lots of book covers for inspiration.

Three Ways Self-Publishers Fail at Cover Design

It's not a small thing to write a book, to actually complete the project. Maybe it's a novel you've worked on for years, going through revision after revision to polish it to perfection. Or perhaps you've put together a book of lessons you've drawn from your life, or a detailed history of your hometown.

You've had to organize your thoughts and your writing, make sure the book is consistent. If you plan to sell your book in retail stores, you've probably hired an editor to fine-tune your manuscript. Now it's time to send it into the world, and the first thing people will see is your book cover.

But for a lot of self-publishers, getting their book cover done presents serious challenges. I've organized these challenges into three different types. Let's take a look and see where the problems lie.

1. *The author takes it too personally.*

    Is it a book, or is it your first-born? With some authors it's difficult to tell. We want our books to make a good impression, but the cover of the book is not actually part of the text at all. It is a wrapper that's consumer-product packaging, advertising and market positioning all rolled into one.

    The cover of a book has several critical roles to play, but they usually don't include being a representative of the author's artistic ability, a way to crystallize his vision of the inner life of his characters, or a way to show his favorite colors. None of these elements, no matter how strongly they reflect the author's style or beliefs, has anything to do with creating a cover that works well for your book in the marketplace.

2. *The author thinks the cover doesn't matter that much.*

I'm guessing that this is the reason for many of the book covers I've seen on self-published books. If the author is following a gameplan, these covers look like something done so that a box could be checked off. "Okay, cover, got that done in 6 minutes with this snazzy book cover template thingy!"

Many subsidy publishers have cover template creation software on their websites. While this approach can rescue the very worst covers from a bad fate, they inevitably end up looking like all the other covers churned out by the same machinery. In a market flooded with over 1,000 new books a day, this is not a solution that will help your book.

3. *The author doesn't understand her book's genre.*

It's funny the way we develop ideas about how things should be. An author trolling the aisles at the local Border's sees a best-selling book with an attractive cover. He thinks, "I'll just make my cover like this, that will work." But notice something: the book he's looking at is a novel about the hijinks nannies get up to in New York City. His book is about retirement communities in the Southwest.

The author, caught up in a good looking book from a big publisher, has forgotten that the people who will buy his book have almost no overlap with the people who buy the nanny book.

Why We Go Wrong

In every one of these cases the aspiring publisher has made basically the same mistake. They forgot that the book cover is the responsibility of the book publisher.

What I mean to say is that becoming a self-publisher means making the transition from an author to a business person. It means that you have to become mentally agile, able to "switch hats" at a moment's notice. The author is concerned with self-expression, style, voice, and consistency.

The publisher is concerned with product development, marketing, making a profit. The publisher looks at the book cover as one of the chief selling tools she has in her arsenal, the face the book will display everywhere, on store shelves, in online listings, in book catalogs and book reviews.

Even the title of the book comes under examination by the publisher. Is it a title her market will understand? Will it communicate quickly and clearly the book's *unique selling proposition*? Will blurbs on the cover help sell books?

How to Get It Right

We can get these decisions right if we remember which role we're playing at any moment. When the writer hands the book's packaging and production over to the publisher, she needs to let go. It's the publisher's responsibility to know the market, to know the other books in that market, and to understand how to position her book appropriately.

At this point the publisher may decide that the best business decision she can make for the ultimate profitability of her book is to call on a book designer and work in collaboration to design the book. But whatever decision she makes, if she keeps the roles of author and publisher separate, she's more likely to make a good decision for her book.

When authors become self-publishers they need to step into a new, less personal role with the book they have nurtured. It's in the best interests of the book's profit potential for the key decisions to be made with its market in mind. Titles and covers are, essentially, marketing decisions.

What Book Designers Do to Get Your Self-Published Book Into Print

I frequently get asked what exactly a book designer does. Just the other day I spoke with a client whose book is in copyediting. I'll be getting ready to start work on his interior next week.

"Well, you don't need to do much," he said. "I mean, you just stick the page numbers on the pages, isn't that about it?"

I couldn't help but laugh. "I guess we must be doing our job pretty well," I replied, "if you can't even tell the difference from one book to the next."

But I got to thinking about it later. We talk frequently about the need to hire publishing professionals, to get your book properly edited and designed to compete in the marketplace or, if you're going to do it yourself, to make sure you understand the conventions and best practices of book production.

When a Designer Is Not Just a Designer

But there are book designers and book designers. Many cover designers do only covers, that's their specialty. Some designers do only interiors. There are designers that do covers, websites and marketing collateral. Then there are designers who provide a complete resource for self-publishing authors.

When I meet with prospective clients the first time, it's really the beginning of a relationship. In this relationship we share responsibility for the embodiment of their manuscript in the form of a consumer product. By the time the books roll off the press, I may have been involved in many aspects of the book's development.

Recently I sat down and made a list of 22 tasks that fall to the book designer in the course of a project:

1. Determine whether the prospective self-publisher can articulate a clear goal for her book and, if not, to help her achieve that.

2. Help the client determine the category, niche, or target market for the book.

3. Assist client in obtaining ISBN, LCCN, SAN and publisher listings if needed.

4. Help the client select the best printing process to meet their goal and find an appropriate provider.

5. Analyze the formats that will be needed in the finished book.

6. Arrange for copyediting, if the author has not done so already.

7. Set up a production schedule.

8. Hire an illustrator if needed.

9. Clean up text files submitted by author.

10. Create sample interior designs, using a representative chapter and most if not all of the formats needed for the final book.

11. Create sample cover designs demonstrating the different ways the book can be positioned within its category.

12. Work with client to adjust designs to fit their needs and aesthetics.

13. Layout all the pages of the book, correct formatting where needed and adjust the length to the right number of pages.

14. Remind the client to finish the copy for the copyright page.

15. Obtain a spine width calculation, cover template and technical specs from client's book printer.

16. Layout and proof the complete flat cover including barcode.

17. Scan photographs if necessary, and adjust photographs for selected printing method, if any are used.

18. Prepare Advance Review Copies (ARC) for marketing and review purposes.

19. Arrange for proofreading and indexing if needed.

20. Advise publisher about her packing, shipping and storage options for offset books.

21. Create reproduction files conforming to printer's specifications, and coordinate proofing and production with printer.

22. Celebrate every milestone as one step closer to the client's goal.

If It's a Real Production, Am I a Producer?

When I looked at this list, I realized why my favorite term for what I do is *Book Producer*. However, no one has ever called me up saying, "I need a book producer," so I don't use it. But that's what it is, gathering the resources and talent needed to produce the book at hand, and making sure the project runs smoothly, and on budget, to a satisfying conclusion.

Keep in mind that nothing in the list of 22 tasks above describes the biggest part of the designer's work: creating the typographic container for the author's work, and doing the actual fitting, pushing, nudging, aligning, sizing and organizing of the content into something that looks the way a book should look, that actually enhances the experience of reading.

And that, in the end, is really the most satisfying part of what I do. Most of the books we create, even if they are influenced by the fashion of the day, will be around far longer than we will. As a designer sometimes I feel as if I stand between the 500-year traditions of bookmaking on one hand, and the potential hundreds of years some of these books may last on the other.

Not a bad place to be at all.

The Death of Book Design

Book Design. (1452 – 2011). Born near Mainz, Germany, Book Design came of age in the heady atmosphere of Venice in the Italian Renaissance. He went through a rocky adolescence when he seemed to lose track of his roots, but matured into the confident and gracious Book Design of the twentieth-century's Golden Age of Letterpress.

He grew up among the presses of his uncle Aldus Manutius, fetching lampblack and sharpening stones for Francesco, the punchcutter in the back of the shop who was always busy fashioning new typefaces to keep the levers on the big presses cranking.

Later he got caught up in a rough group, and spent his youth in the company of a delinquent named Billy Caslon and his henchman, Smooth Johnny Baskerville. Book Design barely escaped this period with his ligatures intact.

In the fullness and power of maturity, Book Design was infected with the deadly *photo-offset* virus. Undermining the connection between metal type and the pages of books, the virus slowly sapped the life from Book Design until, in his delirium, he could no longer resist the siren call of arbitrary placement on the page, quick and easy changes to basic layouts, and the promise of color, color and more color.

The virus was eventually brought under control, and Book Design entered one, final productive period of life. In an explosion of creativity in which old forms and standards were enlivened by the new offset techniques, Book Design reached an acme of achievement in the creation of books.

He learned to bring the disparate elements of typography and photo-lithography into harmony, achieving an often stunning frontispiece to his reality. All was well once again in the world of Book Design.

However, it would not last long. Book Design finally succumbed to a far deadlier virus that swept the world, infecting everything: *digitization*. Objects—formerly a part of the real world—slowly decayed into a series of "1"s and "0"s (whatever they are). Book Design was no different from Music, Art, or even Typing.

The infection proved to be too much. When it was discovered the virus was of the deadly *verdana* variety, hope was essentially lost. As the world watched, Book Design's ePub count was rising dangerously fast.

As fonts—the basic building blocks of life—began to bend and warp under the pressure of digitization, *the book itself* wavered and then collapsed.

In the final stages of this deadly disease, ePubs take over the bookstream, and books lose everything that had made them books to begin with. Book Design's paper wasted away, and the covers that everyone had so admired faded to a collection of unreadable moire patterns.

One night, little noticed by any of his friends, under a Smashwords moon, Book Design breathed his last. He had dropped his serifs and was gone.

Oh, some say he was out where he shouldn't have been, looking for a pixel he could love, when he fell into some sort of meatgrinder and that's what killed him. But it's just a story people tell to scare the little ones.

Book Design had been sick and losing density for many years. His ppi count was way down, and he was showing stress around his spine.

It's no wonder. All the smiling sadists with their instruments of torture, their Kindles and iBooks, their Nooks and Tabs, had been unleashed on his body. Right in public, on busses and in coffee shops, they crushed and stretched his text, madly changing from Arial to Verdana to Baskerville and back again, viciously reflowing his insides over and over. It was just too much for his system to bear.

When a little menu popped up offering to change an entire book to Cochin in one instant, friends of Book Design knew the end wasn't far off.

Book Design is survived by his stepsons, Digit Al Typography and E. Books.

There are rumors occasionally that Book Design has been sighted here or there in an old barn in Derbyshire, or off the coast of San Francisco, but no conclusive proof has ever been offered. The trade in so-called relics, like the phony Folio of Fortunata, with its promise of perfect alignment and infinite registration, are nothing but hoaxes perpetrated on the weak-minded.

In lieu of fleurons, donations can be made to the Old Typographers Rest Home and 24-hour Internet Cafe.

R.I.P.

Designing Books

I've tried to explain to people why I enjoy designing books, but somehow descriptions elude me. When I talk about it, it never comes out right. But here I'm going to try again.

Right now I'm designing three books for different clients, all in distinct genres whose requirements and expectations vary. Like sketching with a pencil, the sample designs that I'll create for these books represent *possibilities* more than established *historical fact*. They exist for me in a world of latency. Before any decisions are made, all the designs are possible, but only one design will eventually embody the complete, published work.

Into this field of possibility I pull the elements of the book together. Text, image, structure, typography: they are the ingredients, but I'm still discovering the recipe. I move the elements around. I'll tell you what I'm doing, even though I know it will sound strange: I'm trying to discern what these ingredients want to be, where they fit together.

It's Like a Dance

One of the books I'm working on is self-help. Another is a book of poetry.

The third is all in formal spreads, a horizontal format, photographs facing short texts. Each spread is a tableau, the repetition as you turn the pages reinforces the formal roles each element plays. Typefaces become critical because the abundant white space will thrust the type design directly into the reader's field of view.

Subheads slide to the left, slide to the right, float up and down looking for their spot, the place they contribute best to the whole layout. Typefaces appear, only to be replaced by others. Images shrink, stretch, run off the pages. Everything is fluid, malleable, but most arrangements feel wrong.

If this was an article with bullets and numbered lists, I would enumerate the different conditions that vary while the design is forming. But it isn't, because the process I go through is much less direct than that.

Actually laying out books after the design is set is an entirely different type of work. Marketing on Twitter, following conversations on blogs I admire, writing Design Reviews for Self-Publishing Review, running invoices and doing bookkeeping—they are all different. Here, I'm open to the stream of possibilities, new connections that I sense around me, even if I usually forget they are there.

Sometimes this whole process is wrestling, sometimes it's a dance. Sometimes I have no idea what's going on, and sometimes I get bored out of my mind. Then I have to get up, stretch, walk away, connect with another human, just to bring myself back to life.

It's All About the Book

Something happens, the pages start to take shape, the page elements begin to settle down, find their place. A form emerges that uses all the elements to advance the book, not suck energy away from it. Something new, something I hadn't seen about the writing, often shows up during this phase.

Throughout the process the author is my companion. I need to have an idea what's behind her writing, where she's coming from.

When the book clicks in, when the author (or the publisher) and I come to a consensus on the final layout, I can almost feel how the energy flows, unimpeded, from the manuscript to the reader, delivered by the typographic design. Something inside me has reflected the ideas in the book and embodied them in the design. Helping the text connect with readers while getting out of the way of that connection.

At the same time, I realize that the page designs I'm working on come together in an idealized form. They exist only on my screen, where they emerge, the software's tools lying around as if my screen were a book *garage*, and me the mechanic. But the page achieves a kind of seductive perfection on screen that really is an idealization of its other life.

No, it will be much later, when the corrugated shipping package arrives, scuffed from its travels, and I slice it open on the counter—that's when reality runs backward for me. I look at the printed book, feel the weight of it in my hand, smell the paper, the fresh glue, and notice the little imperfections that are inescapable in *physical* life. Then it almost seems as if the book I'm holding *caused all the actions* that brought it here, into being.

I have a shelf for these samples and, after my examination, it will join its mates. But first I'll see whether the chapter openings worked as well as I'd hoped, I might wish I had added some space here or there, or argued one last time with the author about how those bullet lists should look.

But not for long. There's a memoir by a Vietnam veteran, the first chapters just arrived, and I have an idea for the page layout I want to try . . .

Social Media for Authors

Rise of the Content Creators

A lot of our culture works on the *blockbuster* model. You put out lots of books, or movies, or records, knowing that most will fail to repay your investment. But you don't mind, because you only need that one blockbuster that delivers huge sales to fund the whole roulette game for another season.

In April, when Smashwords.com e-books first appeared in Apple's iBookstore, Mark Coker, the founder of Smashwords, wrote:

> "Very few people in the publishing industry understand the profound implications of this. It's not just about the iPad – it's about how any author, anywhere in the world, can go from a Microsoft Word document to worldwide e-book store distribution in a matter of seconds or days."

The blockbuster model is under attack, especially in the online world. At first digitization was slow, affecting big culture and big media only peripherally. But by keeping the internet open, free, untaxed and mostly unregulated, the apparently innate desire of many people to produce content became a reality.

In May, self-published thriller author JA Konrath responded to a question on his blog:

> "The dominance of e-books is coming. I have no doubt. But I always thought it was the readers who would lead the charge, based on cost and convenience. Now I'm start-

ing to believe that the ones with the real power are the ones who should have had the power since the beginning of publishing. The ones who create the content in the first place."

Every advance online has made content easier to create and easier to share. Just in the last couple of years it's become mundane for a person to create a decent-looking video, write up a bunch of copy, create a podcast and post it all to the web, sharing it with anyone who cares to investigate it.

Media critic Ken Auletta, in his *New Yorker* piece in April, said:

"Ultimately, Apple is in the device—not the content—business," the Apple insider said. "Steve Jobs wants to make sure content people are his partner. Steve is in the I win/you win school. Jeff Bezos is in the I win/you lose school."

The growing mass of content creators exploded with the advent of easy-to-use social media. At the same time, books became digitized and reproducible in ways never before imagined. Tens of thousands of people are now taking over the publishing functions that have been tightly held for generations. Journalism, publishing, opinion, music, video, reviews, news are all open now, in a way they were never open before, to exploitation by an enterprising individual.

Frank Bell, in *Entrepreneur* (from the Microsoft Small Business Center):

"Most of the fastest-growing sites on the internet now are based on user-generated content. Their popularity has grown tremendously over the past couple years. There are many new opportunities for aspiring entrepreneurs in this area. . . . Overall, user-generated content is creating a medium where masses can interact and has become an incredibly powerful force across the web."

A latecomer to the party, I've been struck by how much the online world resembles my fantasy of the wild west. There are still huge swaths of land to stake out, competition is fierce, but opportunity is as big as it has ever been. Even the recession has played a role by creating demand for cheaper, digitized forms of content.

In June, James Woollam, Managing Director of F+W Media International, wrote on Futurebook.net:

"For most nonfiction publishers much of our content will slice into smaller, more easily digested, pieces. If I think of a . . . craft book, they are mostly project-driven and there's no reason why they wouldn't slice into individual or grouped projects which could sell at a lower price point. It's easy to see how this would apply in DIY, gardening, travel etc."

We see people desperately trying to hold on to the old model. where hierarchies of interest and persuasion control access to media. No matter how this free-floating, fast-changing field changes, it seems unlikely people are going to go back to being passive consumers of content.

In June, Michael Learmont wrote in *Advertising Age Online*:

"David Eun, president of AOL's media and studios division, said he had . . . come to one overarching conclusion: produce more content, faster."

Will we get to some point, like the threatened Social Security Trust Fund, where there are so many people producing content on so many topics at every hour of the day, that there simply are not enough people left to actually read, watch, or listen to the content? Is a lot of the content being created today going to go *readerless*?

According to BlogPulse.com, today:

"Total identfied blogs: 126,861,574 | New blogs in last 24 hours: 42,234 | Blog posts indexed in last 24 hours: 1,178,334"

Did you know that William Shakespeare, one of the most famous playwrights (content creators) of his day, and the most celebrated in history since his death, left not one manuscript in his own handwriting, perhaps only one convincing signature from his own hand, and not one authentic likeness?

And what about us? What new world of information are we creating with our content? Does what we say have a real reason for being said?

I think a lot of it does. My father was a master compositor, a journeyman printer. I can close my eyes and watch his square, capable hands nudge a piece of brass 1/72nd of an inch thick into position next to a line of type, watch him lock up a form that looked like a 3rd-grader's construction project, yet hummed like a tuning fork when he struck it with his battered quoin key, ready to go on press. He could handle paper, jog and score it perfectly each time. He had many skills—but he passed away. Like most of the people who've come before us, all the accumulated wisdom went with him.

If all we do is leave a record of what we know, *what we know how to do really well*, I think we will have done a good thing. And self-publishing will be the route that many of us take to create that record.

The Hub and Outpost Method to Organize Your Social Media Marketing

Most authors have gotten the message: you have to be marketing on social media sites if you want to make an impact and, eventually, sell your content.

Social media is indispensable to today's self-published authors, but it's good to remember that social media by itself is one tactic in your overall marketing strategy. Just using social media is not a strategy in itself; it's a way to implement your basic marketing thrust.

Set Up Your Hub

This method of organizing your social media activity (and thanks to bloggers Chris Brogan and Darren Rowse for this concept) requires that you set up a Hub that will be your home base. It could be a blog or a website. What's important here is that you own it. You own the domain name, it doesn't belong to another entity the way that blogs on blogspot.com or wordpress.com are part of a larger company. You need a place over which you exert ownership, which you can control without worrying about other people's terms of service.

Here are a few good reasons to use your blog as the hub of your social media strategy:

Your blog is frequently updated—This is the place it's easiest to post new material relating to your book or your subject area, and consequently is the most up to date and flexible site you have.

Your blog has your list opt-in—One of the reasons you want visitors to stop at your blog is to find the people who are interested enough in what you're doing that they want to stay in touch and hear more from you. Your newsletter or mailing list opt-in form should be prominent on your blog, and you also should offer subscriptions to your blog via email or RSS, another way to keep in touch.

Your blog is the best place to release news—Blog software allows you to easily post updates or breaking news items, which then go onto your subscribers through the email or RSS feed. It's the best way to stay in touch with your fans and followers.

Your blog is interactive—At your blog you have the best tools for interacting with readers in a robust way over a long term.

Explore to Find Outposts

Outposts depend on your own subject matter and preferences for working, but they have to be places where people interested in your subject congregate.

You might find effective outposts in:

- Facebook fan page
- Twitter accounts
- Forums that deal with your topic
- Photo sharing sites like your stream on Flickr.com
- Video sites like your channel on YouTube.com

- Bookmarking sites like StumbleUpon.com
- Networking sites like Linkedin.com
- Specialized niche sites like those run on Ning.com

Really, there's no limit to the number or type of outposts you create.

At your outposts you might post links to content you've published at your hub. But you'll also contribute content to the outpost sites, too. Outposts are used for:

- listening to what others in your niche are doing
- building authority by contributing expert tips and answers to questions
- testing ideas for marketing or for your next projects
- networking with other people and influencers in your niche
- growing your online profile
- creating links back to your hub

Remember to link to your hub at every outpost. These links create the connections that people will use to travel back to your hub. On Twitter, for instance, the link will show up in your bio, and that will be the first place people click on to find out more about you when they've been intrigued by one of your postings.

Go Forth and Multiply

It's likely that new social media sites with different approaches to connecting people will continue to sprout online. With the hub and outpost model for your social media strategy, it's easy to integrate new locations.

You might decide, for instance, to start building a series of Squidoo lenses about your topic or your book. Linking back to your blog is a natural way for people who come across your sites on Squidoo to find out more about you.

When they travel back to your blog they'll find links to your other sites, like the site you've set up for your individual projects, your content's Facebook fan page, your Twitter account, and you'll be able to supply links and "follow" buttons for all of them.

From this central location, you will rule your (social) media empire. So go forth, creator, and multiply your voice and your influence, confident that you can make use of all that traffic you generate with your insightful comments and spectacular status updates.

How to Get Started on Twitter

Do you have a fear of Twitter engagement? Do you have an account on the service but don't know quite what to do with it? Are you getting ready to publish a book and realize you have to get up to speed with your social media marketing?

A lot of authors I talk to want to learn social media and how it's going to help them sell thousands of books by going viral. But they hesitate, baffled by how the whole thing works. They know they need to be building their author platforms, but don't know how Twitter fits in.

Maybe you don't even need a book to learn it from, since Twitter is a pretty simple platform. There are only a few things you can actually do on Twitter. Everything else that flows from your involvement with it comes from the network of people you connect with.

And in order to connect with the people you want to tell about your work, you have to forget the whole idea of how Twitter will sell thousands of books entirely. Because it won't. Not directly, anyway.

Twitter is powerful, but its power is in connecting to other people, in growing a community around the value of the content and ideas you share. I'm confident you can use it to your benefit if you can only get started.

These are simple things you can do to get going with Twitter, and to learn about what goes on there and how it works.

10 Steps to Getting Started on Twitter

1. *Get a twitter account.* Make sure your username isn't too long, 10 or 12 characters should do. Remember that your username on Twitter, if you're going to use it for promoting your book, is part of your *branding strategy*.

2. *Get some software.* There's great free software that makes Twitter a lot more fun and efficient to use than the official website. I like Hoot Suite on my Mac, Twitterific on the iPad and the iPhone, although there are many others. Get one that appeals to you and fool around with it to see how it works. Being able to schedule Tweets in advance is a big advantage.

3. *Seek out your people.* Do some searches to find the thought leaders and people with the biggest followings in your niche. By finding just one you can start looking through the list of who they are following to find more people to follow.

4. *Find friendly lists.* Twitter lists allow you to create categories of people to follow all at once. For instance, I have a list called "Self-Publishing" with 55 Twitter users self-publishers could follow for great information on the field. Try to find lists created by someone in your field. These are a great place to find people to follow too.

5. *Follow the tweets.* You should now be following many important people in your niche, and you're likely adding followers too. Keep your focus pretty tight at first so you don't overwhelm yourself with input. Read the tweets from these thought leaders and the people with lots of followers. Click through anything that looks interesting to see what they are linking to. Watch espe-

cially for links that get re-tweeted—or passed along—by more than one of the people you're following. Make sure you check out those links.

6. *Keep reading until you get it.* There's no rush. I read tweets for two or three months before I sent out any tweets of my own. Be patient and keep watching and soon you'll see why some people are popular and lots of people want to follow them—because they consistently provide links and ideas that are valuable. Or because they make an effort to connect with people individually. You want to be one of those people, so keep reading until you understand what makes them popular to their followers.

7. *Tweet some value.* By this time you've seen what's considered valuable in the niche you're following. It's time to become a participant. Do a little web surfing and see if you can find resources that haven't been mentioned recently. Create a short tweet alerting people to this resource and put in a shortened link and tweet it.

8. *Follow the golden ratio.* Tweet something of value, or re-Tweet someone else's content or message two or three times for every Tweet you do that promotes your own book or website or other content. This is all about sharing discoveries, sharing content, not about selling. You are building trust and a community of followers at the same time you are receiving value from the people you are following.

9. *Be trustworthy.* I think this is done most simply by giving value, and by not tweeting anything you have not

personally verified for yourself. Trust is the most important element in the community you are building.

10. *Be generous.* Give as much value as you can. Pass along things of interest from others. Create content that has something of value to other people, something that makes their life better in some way. This will be content you're happy to share with your growing Twitter tribe.

Twitter is an amazing phenomenon, considering that each posting consists of only 140 characters of basic text. The creativity, energy and vitality on Twitter are astonishing. It can be a great place to connect to people who are interested in your work, and who in turn will send your message out into their own networks of followers.

Make sure you have something for visitors to look at, to download, to sign up for on your website or blog when they get there. And keep an eye on your analytics. You'll find Twitter is a growing source of traffic and potential book buyers for you if you follow these simple rules.

I think this quote from Zig Ziglar really illustrates how to use Twitter to best advantage:

"You can have everything in life you want, if you will just help other people get what they want."

Happy Tweeting, and let me know how it works.

Self-Publishing Pro and Con(temptuous)

Just when you think the fires have gone out, they flare up somewhere else. I recently read an article at Rachelle Gardner's *Rants and Ramblings* called "Think Hard Before Self-Publishing?"

Rachelle, a literary agent with a specialty in the Christian market, was advising a correspondent that due to the difficulty of getting distribution, reviews, major media, and because it took time and money to self-publish, it wasn't the right path for everyone.

Rachelle, of course, is part of the traditional publishing landscape, and says as much on her blog. All the points she made were reasonable topics of discussion, and she has a pretty balanced approach to the subject which obviously doesn't interest her that much.

No, the real story to this article is what happened next. Many commentors—there were over 80 comments on this blog post—talked about their take on self-publishing. Some said they might decide to self-publish at some point in the future.

But there was also a large group of writers who expressed an amazing variety of contempt for self-publishing, and for the people who do it. Here are just some of the comments, taken word for word:

"Buyer beware"

"... writers not having the patience to seek agents/publishers and then wait for answer"

"... will not only end up depressing you, it will waste away the time that you could be writing... "

"I think it's a scam. You can't buy acceptance... "

"they believe anything that means they don't have to be evaluated, judged and potentially rejected is a good thing ... "

"for me, it would be giving up, or taking the matter into my own hands. SO I'll write, work hard, and keep plugging along ..."

"I was surprised how many aspiring writers believe that THEY KNOW BETTER than agents or editors... "

"they, in their arrogance, believe all that editors do is "stifle their muse"... "

"they don't see their flaws and think too highly of their skills..."

"it seems to be a place authors go when they can't produce the quality to attract an editor, they don't want to take the time to improve their craft ... "

"I don't have enough ego to believe I know better than editors who pick and choose who to publish for a living..."

"most of the reading public won't pay real money for a self-pubbed book..."

"I've found that those who self-publish are rarely any good at their craft and very often are living in a fantasy land..."

"I will exhaust all other options, or die trying, before I will self pub ... "

"I am praying it never comes to self-publishing for me..."

And In the Other Corner...

The very next day, over on the other side of town, Alan Rinzler published an article on his blog, The Book Deal, called "How Self-Publishing Can Lead to a Real Book Deal."

Rinzler, a legendary editor, gives his credentials on his blog:

> For more than 15 years, I've been Executive Editor at Jossey-Bass Publishing in San Francisco, an imprint of John Wiley & Sons in New York. Prior to that, I was director of trade Publishing at Bantam Books, Vice-President and Associate Publisher of Rolling Stone Magazine ... Simon and Schuster ... Macmillan ... Holt ... the Grove Press."

Sorry for the editing, it just went on and on. Rinzler is also responsible for acquiring books for Jossey-Bass

Here's how Rinzler begins his piece:

> A successfully self-published book can propel you down the road to a book contract at a commercial publishing house.

That's the truth of the matter, despite the worries I hear from writers that self-publishing could doom their hopes of ever landing a real book deal. Don't listen to those persistent rumors and urban myths that agents and editors won't take on books the authors have published themselves.

He goes on to tell the stories of two self-published books he just acquired for Jossey-Bass, and tells about a self-published novelist who got picked up by a literary publisher. Rinzler flat out states his position on self-publishing in no uncertain terms, when he says he's a strong advocate of self-publishing and explains why.

How to Make Sense of it All

How can we have such completely opposite outpourings within the space of 24 hours? Is there any possibility of reconciling the people who have dedicated their lives to snagging an agent, an editor, a book deal, with the Executive Editor out looking for books that have been "successfully self-published" in order to acquire them?

Two things leap out at me from these opposing sides of the issue. The writers who have staked their writing life on getting a contract from a traditional publisher seem to have romanticized the process. They have so much invested in getting that contract, and the validation that goes along with it, the mere existence of self-publishers seems to threaten them.

Self-publishers are people who have, by definition, abandoned the course these "devotional" writers are on. They have strayed from the path, abandoned the true religion and are, consequently, treated almost as heretics, apostates who must be ostracized, rejected by the "real" writers.

On the other hand we have the pragmatic Rinzler, a man who has to fill his list several times a year, and an expert at recognizing quality books that will sell. He includes in his article a list of the "Top four reasons self-published books get signed up." It's all about eliminating risk.

As far as Rinzler is concerned, the self-published author who is successful at selling books is a great prospect for a publisher. She has already proven to have a platform, to be able to sell books, and to have the entrepreneurial gumption to stick with it.

When you finish reading Rinzler's piece, you feel like the self-publishers are the crafty ones, having kept control, kept the lion's share of profits, and kept their options open while avoiding the frustration and delay of endless queries.

If we back up for a minute I think it's clear to see that some books benefit from the resources a large publisher can bring to their publication. There are other books that don't have any need of big media and 3,000-store book launches. The decision on how to publish ought to be made based on what is in the best interests of the individual book, and the author's goals. That's it.

Of course there are self-publishers who are bad writers, and who are deluded. Notice that Alan Rinzler is looking for books that are "successfully" self-published. If he could see some of the books I'm working on right now, books by marvelous authors who have spent a lifetime learning their craft, from part-time writers with a natural gift for a story, to academics who know exactly how a book is put together. Books that have been fact-checked, thoroughly and carefully edited, books whose pages will sing with beautiful typography. If he could see those, I think he just might make an offer on a couple of them. I really do.

Although many people still harbor a sad prejudice against self-publishers, the reality is that self-publishing can be both a joyous expression of personal creativity, and a canny business move. An author's goals and the nature of her book should decide the best path to publication.

---

17 Ways for Writers to Publish Their Content

As self-publishers we usually think of books as the primary way we distribute our ideas, our stories, or our teaching—in other words, our content. Books certainly are the best delivery vehicle for long content, for collections from a variety of writers, or for explaining complex ideas and providing a text to study over a long period of time.

In this age of chunked content, re-purposed content, and the many different ways to re-use your old content, there are more ways than ever to publish interesting, educational or entertaining ideas.

You know that the internet, blogs, article sites, multimedia presentations and many other online formats make use of text in different ways. The flexibility of e-books also clearly shows that the text we prize so highly is still data, and can be manipulated in lots of ways. Each of these formats represents another channel through which you can let people know about your ideas, your books, or your community.

It just makes sense to explore these content channels. When you get a link back to your website or blog you're not only spreading your ideas, but enhancing your traffic. If you are selling from your website, either directly or indirectly this will also affect your bottom line.

It's unlikely that anyone could make use of all these different ways to publish content, but it's amazing how many of them might fit with the subjects you're writing about now.

1. Printed book—the standard-bearer for long text for the last 500 years, looks like it still has life as a text delivery system.

2. E-book—the future of text, according to many. Common workflow today is to prepare the print book first then use the final text to generate e-books in multiple formats for use on different readers.

3. App(lication)—the rise of the app stores has created another opportunity for publishers. Whether you just package your book as an app, or incorporate some of the functionality of today's smart phones, you gain access to tens of millions of smart phone owners, a vast new market.

4. Audiobook—recording someone reading your content gives you access to people who like to listen, rather than read, for enjoyment or education.

5. Serialization—A favorite for fiction writers for a couple of hundred years, issuing your story in episodes can present a long story in bite-size chunks, making it easier to approach for today's attention-challenged readers. And a great way to use social media status updates.

6. Blog—writers are constantly being exhorted to start blogs, build their audience and thereby spread their message. Blogs also thrust your content into the social media space, where readers can give you instant feedback.

7. Articles—article sites like ezinearticles.com aggregate articles you can take from your book, or which you write with an eye on keywords and web traffic, allowing you to passively spread your message, and links to your website, throughout the web.

8. Teleseminar—this audio format using either telephone lines or teleconferencing software creates a de facto classroom in which you or a panel of speakers discuss ideas and take questions from the audience.

9. Webinar—similar to a teleseminar but with video and visuals, webinars are becoming increasingly popular as a means to connect with interested readers and deliver your content with the addition of slides or other visual aids.

10. E-course—delivered primarily by email, an ecourse presents your ideas or instruction on a particular topic one lesson at a time. This is a robust and growing form of at-home training and education.

11. Workshops—gathering a group of students at a physical location, workshops give you the chance for one-on-one interaction with students and may vary from just a few people to hundreds of attendees.

12. Free reports—using one piece of your content as a freebie, perhaps in exchange for an email opt in, will help spread your message even farther. Sites such as Scribd.com and Smashwords.com give you a global platform for distributing your ideas this way.

13. Infographics—some ideas, processes or new ways of looking at existing data can be incorporated brilliantly

into a graphical presentation. If your infographic becomes popular, it can easily go viral and spread to a huge audience.

14. Interviews—the question-and-answer format of interviews can be very useful for giving potential readers a good idea of what you are writing about. And interviews inject a welcome personal element that allows those readers to appreciate you on a personal level.

15. Animation—do-it-yourself animation tools can help you put your ideas into a form that more people may appreciate. Videos like Zoe Winters "Zoe Who?" videos reach audiences that may never have seen your book.

16. Web video—establishing your own Youtube.com channel and issuing videos that describe common applications of your ideas, or in which you read from your book and answer questions, for instance, gives you yet another way to connect to those people who would rather watch than read.

17. Speaking engagements—as an author you are already an expert in your niche. New processes or new ways of thinking about things can easily become the basis for motivational or educational speaking opportunities, content you can adapt from your book.

That makes seventeen ways you can slice, dice, stir-fry and serve your content to whole worlds of readers who may not have heard of you before.

So many of these venues for content are new, unleashed by the power of the internet to connect people with similar interests. It's undeniable that even more methods of content publication will be coming as web 2.0 matures.

Why Authors Shouldn't Blog Their Books

Do you think authors should blog their works in progress? I think, in a lot of cases, it's a really bad idea.

Sure, you can write a book from a blog, and there are kinds of books that lend themselves to being assembled in pieces from blog articles. Books you could write with outlining software, like instructional manuals, might be good candidates for blogging as you write them, because you could get feedback from your readers to help improve the book.

And yes, I know authors who blogged the material for their books and later assembled the manuscript. It seems to work best for journals, episodic memoirs, cookbooks, books that are essentially in "chunks" already due to their nature.

But there are a lot of reasons to think twice about blogging your book.

Author blogs are receiving a huge amount of attention at the moment, and why not? With the incessant calls for authors to get involved online, to ramp up their author platform-building, a blog is central.

Blogs give authors a way to attract readers. A way to connect with those readers. And a way to interact with readers more directly than anything except meeting them face to face, like at a bookstore event.

But there's another side to blogging that authors have to consider as well: Writing a blog is not like writing a book. Let me cut right to the chase:

Blogging is specialized writing—Blogs are almost all written to attract readers who scan headlines looking for a quick read. The headline is, arguably, the most important part of a blog article, and there are numerous online courses, tutorials and how-to's devoted to learning the art of headline writing. But when was the last time you read a book full of headlines? There seem to be three possibilities for writers here: Write what you like and, if you're truly exceptional you may grow a following. If you're just good, you're likely to have very few people reading. Or write articles intended to draw people to your site. But then you're running a small-business blog as an author.

Blogging needs lots of formatting—Every writer on blogging and blog style urges writers to break up long copy, to use frequent subheads, to insert bullet lists. And the numbered list format is ubiquitous in blogging. But all these incessant lists, which work wonderfully one at a time, don't make very good long-form reading. It's fatiguing Would you want to read a book that was full of lists, bullets and highlighted text? I've seen books assembled this way from blog posts, and it's a real challenge to make them readable. Chunking text may be good for blogging, but it works against most book formats. Many of the articles in this book, in fact, which originated on my blog, have been cleaned up and reformatted to better fit the book format.

Blogs are mostly written in either a commercial or a journalistic style—The vast majority of bloggers are writing lifestyle blogs, criticism, current affairs, product reviews, making money, diet or fashion blogs or personal reflections. The short, punchy personal essay has had a remarkable resurgence in the blog world. A 500-word article with one main point, a few bullets and an intriguing headline will work well on a blog. But where exactly does this kind of writing fit into the book you are working on?

Blogs are about communication—A blog is the most common form of social media. You write, and invite others to participate in the conversation you start. But when you're deep in trying to find the flow to your book, or following a meandering narrative path, you may not want any input from anyone else. The conversation you have with your deep nature is far more important during the formative stages. Later, once your work is getting to a final stage, you might get a lot more from sharing with your readers.

Blogs need a schedule—Most successful blogs post articles on a schedule. It's a publication schedule, and regular readers come to expect a blog post at the usual time. But creative work often doesn't cooperate with weekly or monthly schedules. You might write in circles before coming to the core of what you want to say. The pressure to post could lead you to commit to material before it's ready. The schedule alone, although it might work for some writers, could inhibit your creativity in the end.

So by all means have a blog, it's almost essential now, especially if your primary method of selling your books is online or through social media. Use the blog to attract potential readers and also to have fun. And give it time to grow: your blog will repay you with real value, both as the center of your online community, and as an intrinsic part of your marketing efforts.

The Big Problem With Blogging Your Book

There are lots of different kinds of author blogs, just as there are lots of kinds of authors. And there are many ways for authors to approach blogging as part of building an author platform. For instance, you can write a blog:

- that's a personal communication between you and your readers. Particularly if you already have a following, this is a great way to engage with your audience.

- that adds timely or additional information to the subject you wrote (or plan to write) your book about. As an expert, you can use the authority gained from your book to keep offering useful content to your readers, all the while enhancing your brand.

- with the intention of assembling your blog posts into a book. Writers write—that's what they do. Using a blog to help complete your next book just seems to make sense.

But there are problems with the last type of blog, where you intend to blog your book.

"How to Blog Your Book"

Some writers have advocated using a blog to assemble content for a book. Here's how this scenario works:

1. You create a complete outline of every section of the book you want to write. For this method, you want to break chapters up into "chunks" so the individual pieces aren't too long or too short.

2. You write a headline for each section of the outline.

3. You turn each section into a blog post, using the headlines you wrote as the blog titles.

4. You work through the outline in any order you like, since you know the position of everything in the final book.

5. Presto! You put all the blog posts together in the order indicated by the outline, and you have a book.

Blogging Isn't Book Writing

But there's a serious problem with this plan. A crucial defect. A stumbling block you will be putting in your own way.

Because blogs aren't books, and pieces of books make pretty bad blog articles. So here's the problem:

If you write your blog posts as chunks of your book, your blog will probably fail to attract any significant readership. Your book doesn't need SEO, keywords, bullet lists, numbered lists, pull quotes, intriguing headlines or links. It doesn't need any of the other things we do to create something people actually want to read online. As bloggers we strive to publish content that engages web surfers within the few seconds they will look at our page before moving on.

If you try to make a book out of your blog posts, it will probably be unreadable. A book that's 100,000 words isn't just 100 one-thousand-word blog posts. Books need to develop their content over the course of the entire work. It usually takes a team of people including the author and one or more editors to create a smooth narrative that communicates the author's ideas clearly and consistently. Book readers make a commitment to a book that takes a lot longer than a few seconds.

On one hand you present readers with content that's blog-like but in a book: they're going to be reading a book that's 75% lists, with bullets, bold type and all the other "chunking" tactics. On the other hand you present blog visitors with long prose sections that refer to other parts of a longer text, parts that aren't even visible.

It seems to me you lose both ways.

You can certainly use editing to create the content for a book from blog articles, but that's a long way off from the "blog your book" process.

(It was this conundrum, by the way, that lead me to the process I used to create this book from my blog's archives.)

Self-Publishers and the Social Media Divide

Self-publishing has been around for a long time. Walt Whitman and Benjamin Franklin were both self-published authors from times when self-publishing had no negative connotations.

Social media, on the other hand, is a pretty new phenomenon. Blogging is about ten years old, and the social media space has only become powerfully influential in the mainstream in the last couple of years.

When you see anchors news shows on CNN and networks displaying Twitter posts on huge screens and advertising their blogs in prime time telecasts, you know that social media has become a real force within the larger media world.

The Social Media Divide

Those of us deeply involved with the rapidly expanding world of social media sometimes forget that there are millions of people who don't participate in it, or limit their involvement to Facebook groups and making connections on Linkedin.

When it comes to self-publishers, there's a clear divide on social media. On one side are the authors who primarily sell their books online, who use tools like article marketing, blogging, Twitter posts and all the other ways we seek to drive traffic, engage a community, and sell books.

On the other are the self-publishers who have stayed with traditional marketing, press kits, review mailings, bookstore appearances and all the other ways we've developed over the years to launch and promote our books.

These publishers, when confronted with social media initiatives, are likely to disregard the amazing power of network marketing, which is where social media gets a lot of its juice.

Self-Publishers Who Miss the Point of Social Media

- Think blogging is "giving away my content instead of selling it."
- Consider Twitter "a waste of time—you can't say anything meaningful in 140 characters."
- Write two or three articles and keep submitting them to blogs and article sites, over and over.
- Open Twitter accounts and then send the exact same tweet to their 10 followers, day after day.
- Visit forums only to market new books or announce appearances.

Self-Publishers Who Really "Get" Social Media

- Actually want to interact with interested readers.
- Realize that social media give them access to crucial information they need to succeed in their chosen market.
- See peer-to-peer networking as an important part of their marketing efforts.

- Understand that books are changing, and that change creates new opportunities.
- Are on the lookout for new technologies, new venues and new ways to market their books.

Obviously, these are not iron-clad lists. We're all complex creatures.

And you might say there is a third group, those who use every tool at their disposal, traditional and web-oriented, to maximize their books' sales potential.

Which one are you?

The E-book Revolution

The Problem With "E-Books"

It's the eve of the long-awaited announcement from Apple about its e-reading / kindle-killing / publisher saving / book destroying tablet computer.

In the Twittersphere, the feed has been lighting up with people reporting from Digital Book World in New York, and everyone is looking to the future, trying to discern the horizon line somewhere in the distance.

Over here, where we're still cutting down trees and binding sheaves of paper together, I'm struggling with the last piece of copy for the Book Construction Blueprint that I've been working on.

It's the chapter on "E-Books." Here's my problem: like all truly new and breakthrough technologies, the e-books of today are rudimentary and obviously transitional.

The model for almost all e-books is a printed book original, or an imagined printed book original. What I mean is that we have ported the conventions of bookmaking from the world of paper and board into the digital realm simply for our own convenience. They are signposts, markers that help us orient in this new world.

How Is an E-Book a Book?

Reading through various instructions about formatting e-books, parts of e-books, helpful hints about e-books, it's pretty obvious that the authors are making it up as they go along. All the instructions boil down to one question:

How slavishly does the e-book have to follow the physical conventions of the print book?

But, just for fun, off the top of my head, how is an e-book most definitely not in any way a "book" at all?

E-books have no pages—Pages, the two sides of the leaves of paper that make up a book, are intrinsic to printed books. Although e-books imitate "pages" it's just for our convenience. There is no reason an entire novel in e-book form couldn't be written on one "page" or on thousands of bits of displayed text within a programmed environment.

E-books also have no spreads—Although it seems like I'm repeating myself, this is the heart of the book. When the sheaves of papyrus or linen or wood pulp paper are bound they naturally create two (or more) side-by-side pages, or a spread. What makes a book is the binding, so the spread is really the basic unit of the book, not the page.

Every word in an e-book is equidistant from every other word in the e-book—Any location in the e-book can be connected instantly to any other location in the text through hyperlinks.

The text of an e-book is searchable and subject to computer analysis—Just by entering a search term and hitting the Enter key, you can highlight thousands of occurrences of the term throughout the entire text. Instantly.

There is no need in an e-book for text to be linear—An e-book, like almost all text-delivery systems, presents text in orderly rows of type on discrete, sequential pages, but this has nothing to do with the form of the e-book and everything to do with habits and expectations. We are used to reading text that way, so designers have created a model of the book on the screen. With just a little more work they could and do create models that have no debt to the book, where text is free-form, or timed to appear at intervals, or integrated with other media, or reading in circles if they bloody well want it to.

The form, size and typography of the e-book are adjusted by the devices on which they are presented—I have hanging over my desk a page from a religious text printed in Paris in 1495 by a printer named Ulrich Gering, and I have no doubt that Ulrich himself set up this page and printed it on his pull-lever press. It looks exactly the way old Ulrich designed it to look, and it will never change from his intentions. With many e-books, the user can change the typeface, the typesize and other attributes. The e-reader itself will create the format for the pages and how they are displayed.

The Pull of History Cannot Outlast The Push of New Technology Forever

Eventually, of course, popular e-books will break free of their need to imitate print books. But the force of habit and convention is strong. When first graders are given "kinder-kindles" to learn reading, the transition will be pretty complete. Text has become data. Until then we'll use the printed book as our guide, because it's what we know.

E-books will continue to have "covers" although it's impossible to say what's being covered. Indexing will die off, since in e-books, every word is already indexed. We'll still need a copyright notice, but I've seen texts now that just have a link to a rights notice on a server somewhere. It's like an abstraction of an abstraction.

I don't think the print book will disappear anytime soon, but there's an exciting kind of terror in realizing that we are navigating the uncertain waters of epochal change. When I was growing up, hot metal type was the norm. It was dethroned by the allmighty offset press and photolithography. But in technology, you don't get to dominate for long.

The more I think about it, the more I agree with the remark E.M. Ginger, director of 42-line.com and former managing editor of *Fine Print*, made at a recent meeting of the Bay Area Independent Publishers Association (BAIPA): I'm not sure we've seen a digital "book" yet, and I'm not sure we ever will. Not even from Apple.

Is the Paradise We've Lost the Beautiful Page?

Everywhere you turn people are talking about e-books and the future of book publishing. My explorations of the iPad have landed me in the iBooks app for long periods of time, and deep in Stanza on my iPhone, Calibre on my Mac, and Kindles on the various Kindle reader programs on all these platforms.

But this is certainly the "bleeding edge" of change because it's not that common to see people actually reading e-books down at Starbucks, or hanging around the fountain in downtown San Rafael. No, they are probably reading paperbacks more than anything else. Maybe it's just me, with tunnel vision, who sees e-books and their accouterments everywhere.

Then of course I spend hours working on books for design clients, designing pages and variants, producing cover after cover. But all these designs, and the files into which we pour the final manuscripts, are digital, visible only on screen.

When you've been designing books on a computer for a while, you begin to merge the images on the screen and your visceral expectations of the finished book. In other words, when I look at the spread on my monitor, I'm experiencing a kind of projection of what the finished book will be like.

Books designed this way are sometimes oddly disappointing. They can never be as perfect as their digital representation on the screen, the colors never as bright, the pages never as sharp and square. This is a legacy of the digital age.

Books, and Books

Vaguely disattisfied, I wandered out of my office, and noticed the cabinet where we keep the remnants of my book collection, such as it is. At one time I had collected fine books, but that was many years ago. I had only kept a few favorites. I pulled out two large volumes, cases covered in a printed paper, spines wrapped in vellum.

To be so invented miss w, so come it seems
Once found, which yet unfound most would have
Impossible: yet haply of thy Race
In future dayes, if Malice should abound,
Some one intent on mischief, or inspir'd
With dev'lish machination might devise
Like instrument to plague the Sons of men
For sin, on warr and mutual slaughter bent.
Forthwith from Councel to the work they flew,
None arguing stood, innumerable hands
Were ready, in a moment up they turnd
Wide the Celestial soile, and saw beneath
Th' originals of Nature in thir crude
Conception; Sulphurous and Nitrous Foame

This is the 1926 edition of Milton's *Poems* from the legendary Nonesuch Press. The first volume is *Paradise Lost*, the second *Miscellaneous Poems*. Here's a sample from *Paradise Lost*:

The Nonesuch Press was an interesting experiment in improving books for the reading public. The revival of the book arts that had started near the end of the nineteenth century with the founding of William Morris' Kelmscott Press had produced numerous small private presses dedicated to producing books by hand and at the highest level of design and production.

Francis Meynell founded Nonesuch Press with his wife Vera Mendel, and the noted Bloomsbury writer David Garnett. Meynell thought there was a way to improve books, without the exclusivity and high prices of the artisan presses. Like Kelmscott, they produced tiny editions of 100 or 150 books, each of which commanded extravagant prices.

At the time books were almost all printed letterpress. Letterpress printing, invented by Gutenberg in the fifteenth century, had very nearly been perfected by the twentieth century. Mechanization had brought cheap printing to more people, but the book arts were in decline.

Meynell thought he could bring the two sides of book production together. He set up Nonesuch Press with a hand press, just like the other private presses. But after he had completed designing a book in the handpress model, he turned the actual production of the books over to large, commercial printers.

This Milton, for example, was produced in an edition of 1450 copies, a quantity that no handpress could contemplate.

It was printed by the printing office of Cambridge University Press, and is accompanied by illustrations by William Blake.

A Cutting Edge Design in 1926

You may have noticed that the entire book is printed in italic type. This was an unusual decision even in Meynell's day. The italic handwriting of the Rensaissance was considered one of its great humanistic accomplishments, and it had given rise to the very first italic type, cut for Aldus Manutius, one of the earliest and most influential of the Venetian printers.

When the Linotype Foundry decided to resurrect one of the classic roman typefaces of the time, Francesco Griffo's Poliphilus, they decided to combine it with an italic typeface designed by the papal scribe and type designer Ludovico Vicentino degli Arrighi. The modern italic was given the name Blado, after the printer who had used Arrighi's italic fonts.

Meynell decided, in a stroke of design genius, to cast his entire publication of Milton's poems into the Renaissance, the cradle of modern civilization as well as modern bookmaking. The sturdy Blado italic is not some wimpy slanted typeface playing the role of weak sister to a roman face. Oh no, this is a typeface that needs no roman at all, it's complete in itself.

The Long Winter

I sat down and read a few pages of the Milton. The opening lines of this great English poem still resonate for me, many years removed from English class.

Of Mans First Disobedience, and the Fruit
Of that Forbidden Tree, whose mortal taste
Brought Death into the World, and all our woe ...

It took me back to a winter many years ago, after I got this Nonesuch Milton, when I read through *Paradise Lost*. It was an incredible experience. The paper Meynell used for this edition was specially made, coarse, entirely composed of cotton and linen fiber. It's thick by today's standards, and nobbly. It has such a pronounced texture it becomes part of the reading experience. It shows the bite of the metal type beautifully. You can see a little of this texture in the photo on the previous page.

Note the completely even color of the type, something not that easy to do with this kind of letterpress printing. The whole effect of reading this book is unlike other kinds of reading experiences. The artfulness of the type, the energy of Arrighi's italic and the otherwordly illustrations by Blake combine to bring Milton's words to life in an immediate way.

Back to the Future

As I put the Milton back on the shelf, I realized that it's probably not possible to reproduce books like this one any longer. There are many fine printers at work today, and letterpress printing is more popular than it has been for some time. Typography has enjoyed an explosion of interest and talent in recent years, spurred on by digitization.

But Nonesuch managed to hit a "sweet spot" in book design and production at a time when all the printing expertise in the world was concentrated on letterpress. There simply is no commercial letterpress industry any more, and the big iron letterpresses were long ago melted down, replaced by faster, cheaper offset printing.

Anyway, I had to go back to the survey I was doing of the latest publication for the iPad: a video-enhanced, hot-linked, multi-media text that blinked and pulsed at me from the screen. No matter what speed and convenience we've gained, I couldn't help but feel that we've also lost something in the process.

Is there a role for fine printing in our hurried electronic life? Would any of us take the time to spend a winter reading Milton today?

Digital books, new ways of looking at text, and the toppling of old structures in the book business are pushing us toward the future. A look back at the past can remind us of what our ancestors thought important about the design of books.

Less Expensive, Bite-Sized,
Available for Take-Out: The Book of
the Future

Mark Barrett, the proprietor of Ditchwalk.com, is trying to figure out the ePub and pdf translation processes from the point of view of an author who wants to move his work into the public sphere.

When authors start having to roll up their sleeves and get under the hood of translation software, learning the ins and outs of formatting, you know we are still in a hobbyist phase.

Of course, the whole computer culture is still like this, to some extent. It's not as bad as it used to be, when it was assumed that if you owned a PC you would want a nice leather pouch to keep your wrenches, drivers and chip pullers in.

That culture is still around. Today I had the pleasure of learning just enough about cable modems to purchase one of my very own after the leased job I had from Comcast finally keeled over. Several technicians at Comcast had a bit of a snicker about just how long I'd had the old modem. But if it's under your desk and everything is fine, eight years can pass very quickly.

Anyway, here's what Mark had to say at one point in his progress to publication:

Because the stories I want to publish are straight text, the reflowable ePub format not only meets my needs as an author, but it provides the most transparent reading experience for end users. That's a win-win for me because I don't have to make any trade-offs between my own authorial needs and the end-user reading experience.

In a New York *Times* item this week, Nick Bilton looked at the need to take breaks when reading on screens. V. Michael Bove, Jr., director of the Consumer Electronics Laboratory at the M.I.T. Media Lab, was asked whether e Ink (like the Kindle), full-color LCD screens (like the iPad) or paper offered a better reading experience:

> It depends on the viewing circumstances, including the software and typography on the screen.

And What About those e-Books?

I was in high school when McDonald's opened in my home town. We were forbidden, of course, from going there, but the ban had no effect whatsoever. Burgers that were cheap, so cheap even teenagers could afford them. Great fries. No waiting, no sitting around trying to act like an adult at a table. What could be bad?

Convenience, economy, flexibility. This is what the appeal of e-readers is today. And just as my mother couldn't quite get herself to call McDonald's burgers "food" it's hard to see exactly where the "book" is in the ePub reader world.

Is a book a 500-word blog post? I don't think so. How about a 30,000-word blog post, one long page of text? No, not a book. How about a 21-page PDF file, but one where the vendor has created a neat 3D image with modeling software of the report to make it look just like a book, with a spine and everything. Does that make it a book?

It Sounds Good, What's The Price?

There's always a trade-off. Perhaps Mark doesn't think going to ePub impacts the reading experience. Or maybe typography does play a crucial role in readability, and in subtly tying us to our own cultural history.

The monocultures that grew up around the fast food industry have decimated much of the centuries-old agriculture of the country. Farming and livestock production are now done in what amount to animal factories. The buying power and overwhelming financial growth of fast food and greater food processing ability changed everything we eat and, in the process, changed us.

What about books? The books we've grown up with are mass-produced objects of retail trade. Without the mass-production part, the economics of the business change drastically. When the overwhelming growth of e-books, the intoxicating ability to reproduce them endlessly with no cost and no inventory, and the flexibility of the format that allows the texts to flow into and through various devices, when all these forces reach a tipping point, the book will cease to exist as an item of popular culture.

The change from printed books to e-books will not happen overnight, but it is inevitable. We don't know what trade-offs will be involved, because transitions raise more questions than they answer. But the book will not remain the same.

E-books Today: Futility or Utility?

Indie Author April Hamilton responded to an article I wrote about typeface combinations for book design with a note about e-books:

> "Joel   -
> Those font combintations look great, but I can only shake my head and sigh knowing none of them would survive the conversion to Kindle (prc), iBook (ePub), or most other e-book formats intact—the notable exception being pdf e-books, but that's hardly the most popular format. Sadly, font options are still very, very limited where e-books are concerned.
> E-book, thy name is utility."

April, who performs conversions to e-book formats, knows this ground well. For most e-books, text is one long stream of data, paginated on the fly by the ereading device itself. As soon as your text enters this elastic space, it can be manipulated by users for their own convenience. The font you selected can be replaced, and sizes, line endings, page breaks and other parts of the infrastructure of the book are rendered irrelevant.

Craig Mod, in his great article about e-book reading last year, "Books in the Age of the iPad," argued that the Apple iPad was the first reader to be able to display books with the same kind of accuracy in presenting content that printed books do.

He goes on:

The metaphor of flipping pages already feels boring and forced on the iPhone. I suspect it will feel even more so on the iPad. The flow of content no longer has to be chunked into 'page' sized bites . . . In printed books, the two-page spread was our canvas. It's easy to think similarly about the iPad. Let's not. The canvas of the iPad must be considered in a way that acknowledge the physical boundaries of the device, while also embracing the effective limitlessness of space just beyond those edges.

Trapped in the Past, But At Least There's Something to Read

Looking at the ePub versions of lots of books can be dispiriting to a designer. But we are in a primitive and transitional time for books, and we all know it.

E-books remind me today of character-mode displays of 20 years ago. We ran programs on what were essentially terminals with green screens and a single set of characters. You had to know how to enter command-line code to get anything done. When I brought home my first PC, I spent an hour typing at the C:\ prompt and receiving only this in reply:

Unknown command or filename

From there to Mac OSX, the iPhone and the iPad is quite a journey in itself. But e-books, from what I can see, are still in their infancy.

Partly this is due to the current level of technology, certain to change quickly over the next couple of years. But even more, it's our own longstanding habits and cultural memory that will change next.

Then we won't need sophisticated electronics to spend their energy imitating old books and graceful page turns. Text will escape the need for display as electronic pages, and connect with all the media converging on these mobile platforms like the iPad.

From the time people started to bind together sheaves of paper, creating the first books, until today, text has been displayed in only a couple of ways. And books, the standard unit of text communication, still use materials and operate by rules laid down in the sixteenth century.

Here are a few things I'm looking for in tomorrow's e-book experience:

- Text in pages, and not in pages—there are so many ways text can be displayed that might start from the page/spread metaphor, but then go completely beyond it.

- Text in three dimensions—hyperlinks created the first kind of experience of text in dimensions, where depth becomes a factor. E-books are perfect vehicles for this type of content-layering.

- Flexibility of the display, not just the content—and by that I mean presenting an eInk-type screen like the Kindle when only text is involved, and a high-resolution color screen like the iPad when other media come into play. Why do we have to choose?

- Dynamic graphics that interact with the text—breaking down the wall between graphics and text is something e-books can accomplish in totally new ways.

- Context sensitive, location sensitive, environmentally sensitive—harnessing all the computing power in next-generation tablets and other convergent devices can make text responsive to the reader in many new ways.

So my question is, when will e-books break out of the mold of the printed book? And then what will they look like?

Six Keys to Self-Publishing Success in the Age of the E-book

Okay, so we know the e-books are coming. Figures from the International Digital Publishing Forum show that e-book sales tracked through the book trade skyrocketed to $119.7 million wholesale for the third quarter of 2010. And the holiday season hadn't even started.

Each technical innovation seems to empower self-publishers even more. E-books present a fraction of the financial risk that a run of 5,000 printed books poses. And e-books are perfect vehicles for niche publishing.

Even though it seems there are more books being published than ever before, there's also an almost insatiable desire for information products. Savvy online publishers understand what readers are searching for, and how to come up near the top of those searches.

What are the keys to succeeding in this brave new world? Here's what I see.

- Aggressive Pricing—buyers of e-books, still conditioned by Amazon's "all bestsellers for $9.99" policy, want low prices. Low-low. So some writers are building their platform with free books, books for 99 cents, books under $2.99. This audience has its own expectations. Are there any successful trade e-books for $30?

- Great Content—Let's face it, either your book addresses readers' needs and wants, or it fails. It's your job to make sure your book is good at what it intends to do, whether it's information, how-to, telling a story, or inspiring readers to act. Do you have a unique take on a subject? Authority or expertise? You can't succeed without great content.

- Mastering Metadata—Readers find books now with online searches. Recommendations from your trusted indie bookseller? Not so much, since many of the stores have closed, and the seductive convenience of ordering books from your couch is irresistible to American shoppers. Will your book come up on their search? Metadata—information about your book—is crucial and becoming more so.

- Making Noise—What's your hook, your angle, your Unique Selling Proposition? You have one, right? Some way to stand out from the horde trying to grab the attention of browsers, buyers, readers? You can be counter-intuitive, controversial, or over-the-top promotional. You can be the leading authority in your field, or have an offline following. But somehow you have to get attention or you're lost.

- Robust Platform—All the time you've spent building your author platform—your blog, Face-book presence, Twitter following, Linkedin network, fan club, subscribers, followers—is now going to pay off. Authors with a substantial following online are going to be way ahead of the curve. The e-book phenomenon is totally digital. Your wired, connected, with-it fans are the ones who will tweet you, fan you, and spread your message.

- A Generous Nature—A side effect of social media and online communities is the rise of a culture of generosity. People—marketers—who understand this create more lasting bonds with their readers, and inspire more trust. Being generous with your content, with your pricing, with your time and your engagement with your readers is becoming one of the best signs of who gets it and who doesn't, who will create the communities that will sustain them long-term as the move to e-books continues to gather steam.

As with all large-scale change, we simply have no idea where things are heading at the moment. But these traits will carry you a long way on your social media journey.

The Electronic Life

Why Self-Publishers are Exhausted

Writing is mostly a solitary pursuit. You sit in a room with a computer or a pad of paper. You've set aside this time and use your isolation to write. Although it's best to avoid generalizations, writers by and large tend to be people who are fine spending time by themselves.

This worked well when the publishing model involved finishing your book and then sending it off to agents to try to acquire a publishing contract, at which point your publisher would spring into action to do all those things they do to make your book a reality. Perhaps sales would be strong enough to warrant a second book, or a second edition.

It's Not That Simple Any More, Is It?

Even for novelists this "write, and then sit back until the book tour" way of doing things isn't really working any longer. But when you decide to take the plunge into self-publishing, you will have to throw this model out the window.

As a self-publisher, you have fired the publishing house whose attention you once sought so avidly. You create a company and now you are the publisher. This is intoxicating. If you've been reading advertisements from the big author-services companies (known far and wide, and inaccurately, as "self-publishing" companies) you feel you are only a few steps away from a spot on the best seller list.

Soon, however, you begin to discover the awful truth. When you fired the publisher, you also fired:

- the *editor* who was going to help shape your manuscript into a compelling read, suitable for its genre;

- the *interior designer* who would turn your files into a book that looks professional and that communicates your ideas effortlessly;

- the *cover designer* who creates a highly-polished sales identity and mini-billboard to help your book stand out from the thousands around it;

- the *copyeditor/proofreader* who ensure your book is consistent, conforms to standard usage, and contains no factual or typographical errors;

- the *marketing department* that positions your book within its niche and may have even helped come up with the title;

- the *sales force*, ready to spread across the country to introduce your book to buyers at every level of the retail chain;

- the *warehousemen and fulfillment workers* who store, stack and ship your book to distributors, wholesalers and end users; and

- the *bookkeepers and accountants* who keep track of all the sales, returns, promotional copies and review copies.

I don't know about you, but this list makes me want to have a nap.

Spinning in Circles, Wondering Which Way is Up

It's no wonder that self-publishers are exhausted. Worse, for a novice the sheer mass of information, tips, guidelines, books, websites, blogs, free downloads, ecourses, and expert advice flying at you like the birds in that old Hitchcock movie are enough to make you swoon from information overload, retreat into "paralysis by analysis," or just simply put your head in your hands and weep.

How will you possibly learn enough to do any of the tasks listed above adequately? You become keenly aware that, even if you spend $660 for Adobe InDesign, you are faced with a steep learning curve and no idea of what you are supposed to have at the end of the process. How will you learn all the skills, techniques, contacts, and best practices of all these people who have spent their professional lives learning each aspect of how to publish books?

Case in Point?

Almost every day I get inquiries from prospective self-publishers, and if I could reduce them to one generic question, it would be this: "What do I do now?" A few months ago I spoke with an author who had written a book, gone so far as to find a friend—not all that skilled, as it turned out—to lay out the book in InDesign, and managed to get a proof from a print on demand supplier.

When he got the proof copy of his book from the printer and realized how many errors it had, both typographically and stylistically, he simply threw it on the bookshelf and didn't look at it for months, unable to deal with the mass of work and the expertise it would take to make it the book he had dreamed of publishing.

Don't Let This Happen to You

Don't allow yourself to fall victim to a very destructive idea that can take root soon after you decide to self-publish:

Self-publishing doesn't mean you have to do everything yourself. It only means that you are the publisher. And just as Alfred A. Knopf himself would not have typeset the books his publishing house produced, perhaps you shouldn't either.

Avoid overwhelm, burnout, and weeping in frustration. The solution is to approach your new business as . . . a business! Do what you can do well, and the things that you are interested in. Mostly, you should confine yourself to writing and marketing your book. Leave the rest to the many skilled practitioners who are only too happy to help.

Yes, it will cost more money. Look at this money as an *investment* in the product you are creating. Determine to go into the marketplace with the best book you can afford to create. *Create the book that you originally dreamed of.*

After producing dozens of books for self-publishers over the years, I can't tell you how much happier, and more satisfied, you will be down the road. And isn't that why you decided to create this book in the first place?

I Am My Keyboard

Around the time that the desktop computer started to become a common business appliance, I noticed something odd. As more industries became computerized, I—as a consumer—was being asked to do more of the work that had been done previously by skilled professionals.

- Typing, which became word processing, was once done by secretaries (see *Mad Men*). Now I had to do it myself, on my word processing software.

- Typesetting for books, once done by typesetters, was being done by guys in their dining room on early Apple computers.

- Booking flights, once done by travel agents, was faster and cheaper to do on the web, once the airline's databases were made available.

Where once each task took place in its own world, according to its own rules, using its own material and discussed in its own jargon, now it was all flowing through the computer.

And rather than specialists somewhere doing these things, we had all become computer operators instead of typesetters, secretaries, travel agents. The world was becoming digitized, like one of those scenes from *The Matrix,* but charmed by the new technology and the power it brought to individuals, we didn't realize it.

Away from Reality, Please

To be modern, to take on these tasks, we needed the computer. Everyone wanted one at first. Then, everyone had to have one. Or their boss came in and put one on their desk, and said, here, this is the new way.

- Typesetters who used to pick up little pieces of metal and arrange them in lines, or who operated big noisy machines that cast lines of type in hot metal slugs, now sat and tapped at keyboards.

- A friend, who for years had slaved over a big flatbed film editing machine, cutting and splicing thousands of feet of film, bought a Macintosh and sold the flatbed years ago.

- The car mechanic, who used to listen to the engine and tap various locations on the car with his wrench, now operates a computerized diagnostic machine that tells him what's going on.

The list goes on and on. The checkers at supermarkets used to know all the prices, did you know that? Now, they are scanner operators. London taxi drivers used to study for a year or more to learn the city well enough to pass the license test. I wonder if they slap a GPS on the dash now, and just get on with it.

People who cut fabric for dressmaking operations now feed the information into sophisticated cutters driven by computers and watch as the machine does a far more accurate job than they ever did.

Doctors once used their ears, eyes, hands as well as the knowledge in their heads, to diagnose you. Now, they wheel you onto a tray and shoot you inside a machine that does all the diagnostic imaging, and a technician interprets the images.

Designers, printers, typographers, illustrators came together and pooled their skills and knowledge of design, paper, type, inks, and printing presses, and produced books. Now we upload two files to a server somewhere, and wait for the Fedex to deliver our book.

We have gradually been drawn away from contact with the things of the world. Instead, our experience is *mediated* by the computer, a device for manipulating, creating and transmitting digital data.

Does it matter if we never touch the pile of cloth, the paper, the type, the abdomen of the patient, if we no longer learn the different sounds the engine makes, the feel and taste of the soil, does that matter?

For all the wonders that digitization has brought to the world, there are things that have been lost, that we are losing right now.

I've pulled the long lever on a hulking black iron press, felt the kiss of the inked type against the tooth of the paper. Thousands of pulls, thousands of kisses, and eventually you acquire a "feeling," the sense of what's happening where it cannot be seen. Have we lost the need for the gradual accumulation of experiences like that? Or do we just focus on stuff that's more important now?

I don't know the answer to that question, I just keep asking it.

Frustrated Self-Publisher Escapes DIY Trap

I got caught in the trap. The trap I've warned you about, the trap that waits for anyone who takes control, decides to *be the media* instead of relying on specialists to decide whether our story is worthy, whether it should be published.

Look, there's nothing wrong with doing it yourself. That's what the "self" in self-publishing is all about. I've even written about the trap, because I see it so clearly in my clients and friends who publish books.

I thought there must be a reason. Did I fall into this trap, or was I pushed? I suspected social media.

How Does Your Schedule Look?

I have two jobs: book designer and blogger. Like a lot of others, I'm both a consumer of social media, and a creator of it. I blog. Like you, I spend time on Twitter every day. Okay, I do belong to half a dozen Ning groups, and blog occasionally at several. Yeah, I check my Facebook page every once in a while, and correspond with people through their email system. Sure, I'm building a Squidoo lens and trying to figure out Stumbleupon. Even so, I think I've shown remarkable restraint.

No, the trap I've fallen into wasn't laid by my attraction to social media.

Here's the trap:

When you decide to be a self-publisher, when you decide to "do it yourself," for some reason you subconsciously think that means you have to do everything yourself.

You're the author, and now you want to be the publisher. Does it follow that you have to be:

- The book designer?
- The typesetter?
- The person who writes the press release?
- Sets up the website for the book?
- Plans the book tour?
- Gets printing estimates?
- Edits and corrects the manuscript?

No, of course it doesn't. And how are you going to learn how to do all those things? If you're the studious type, your book may never get published, because you'll still be studying how to set up the margins in InDesign, or studying press release samples, or watching webinars about ePub conversions.

Does this really make sense? Do you want to learn how to style, convert and correct the ePub files for your book, when you are only going to do one book?

This is the trap.

How I Got In, How I Got Out

I've had two books under development myself, in two completely separate niches, and I'd been making exactly no progress on either.

Why? Because I'm the expert, I know how to edit, design, market books. So I should do it myself, right? That's where I fell in, because I have no time to sit down and start editing a couple of hundred pages of transcripts to make them suitable for publication.

But thinking that I *ought to be doing it myself* put me in the situation of not reaching my goal of publishing these books.

When I realized what had happened to my book projects, I almost laughed out loud. I said, to no one in particular, "And I'm the guy people call to find help when they need it!"

I actually experienced a rush of excitement when I thought of turning both these projects over to a couple of the terrific editors I work with, and teaming up with them to get the books ready to publish.

I knew right away this was a winning strategy. Committing the resources upfront would be an investment. I know that as soon as I can get these books onto the market, they will start earning back that investment. The longer I wait, the longer I delay that investment paying off.

Publishing for profit, no matter how big your publishing company, is a business. Success in business arises out of smart, timely use of your resources and an understanding of your market. I had to learn again to switch hats, from being the author, to being the designer, to being the publisher who's in charge of the show.

Now I'm busy looking for other areas where projects are stuck, and how I can find the talent to get them moving. That's exciting.

How can you unstick your business? Do you try to do everything yourself? How is that working out for you?

The 5-Million Word Typewriter and How to Stay Focused

The New York Times recently carried an interesting story about the author Cormac McCarthy and his decision to sell his trusty typewriter, an Olivetti Lettera 32. Here's how Wikipedia cited the *Times* story:

> Cormac McCarthy used an Olivetti Lettera 32 to write nearly all of his fiction, screenplays, and correspondence over a fifty year period from 1960 to 2009. In 2009 the typewriter was auctioned by Christies to benefit the Santa Fe Institute. McCarthy paid $11 for a replacement typewriter of the same model, but in newer condition.

And here's how the *Times* characterized McCarthy's output on the Olivetti:

> Mr. McCarthy, 76, has won a wagon-full of honors including a Pulitzer Prize, a National Book Award and the MacArthur Foundation's so-called genius grant. Books like "Blood Meridian," "All the Pretty Horses" and "The Crossing" have propelled him to the top ranks of American fiction writers.

McCarthy estimates he typed about 5 million words on the Olivetti, and bought it originally when he was headed overseas and wanted a light machine. Since Olivetti specially designed this typewriter for travelers and correspondents, it was ideal.

In fact, the Olivetti was the laptop of its day. It came in a neat zip-up case with a handle to make it easy to carry. And, as it happens, it's exactly the same typewriter I've owned for 30 years, and on which I wrote the first drafts of *Body Types*. Okay, it's not quite the same as *No Country for Old Men*, but still.

From experience I can tell you that this little Olivetti typewriter actually took a fair amount of banging to get through a page. I don't want to go back to the days of erasable paper, white out, and carbon copies. But sometimes I miss the visceral relation to the writing machine, the physical force it took to drive the keys, through their levers, to hit the page.

I could always tell when I'd been writing something that made me angry, or passionate, because the letters would almost punch through the sheet.

Today, at a Starbucks Near You

Turn your attention to the local Starbucks. Perhaps you are an author, working on a rewrite on your manuscript. You've got your trusty iBook, a big cup of coffee, and you're ready to work. You wait to connect to the WiFi signal, and glance around. The girl at the next table has a new MacBook Pro. You know it's twice as fast as your aging laptop, has a bigger screen, runs all the new software.

You look at your old machine a bit wistfully. It takes a while to load your browser, it won't run the newest games or image editing software, and it hiccups once in a while if you've got too many programs running at once. You start to think just how productive you could be if only you had one of those MacBooks.

Isn't that a good reason to get out the Visa card? I mean, it will help you with your work, right?

Stop, in the Name of Work

It's easy to get fixated on the tools we use to do our work as authors and publishers. What's becoming steadily more difficult is staying focused on the tasks in front of us. The story of Cormac McCarthy's typewriter is a story pared down to its essentials. A man, an instrument that helps him write. Period. There is no email, no browser, no games, no blogs, no tweets, no status updates.

I have a picture in my mind in which I'm sitting at the little table I worked on in our apartment in New York, and McCarthy, at the same time, is banging away on his Olivetti. Just the writer, alone, and the blank page. Have we lost something from that time, something that would make our work better today?

We have to remember how to find the path that will take us to the goals we've set for ourselves. Often, these goals are easier to reach when we can filter out distractions and concentrate on the task that we have to do today.

A Suggestion

Although we need our computers to do our work, I have a suggestion: When you're writing, close all your other programs and *just write*. With nothing else going on, you are free to concentrate on one thing. Single-task instead of multi-tasking. Set this time aside for writing and nothing else. I'm betting you'll get a lot more done.

Tribe

People I talk to look at me strangely when the subject of social media comes up. "Facebook," someone might say, grimacing. "My kids do that, I think. Not for me, thanks." A shake of the head.

"Well," I say, "I spend a lot more time on Twitter than Facebook. It's a great way to meet ..."

"What the hell do I want to know what somebody had for lunch?" An incredulous laugh.

These people are not *in the tribe*. The tribe of people connected through the hours spent at a computer, reaching out to other people sitting at other computers. Living rooms. Dorm rooms. Library carrels. Internet cafes. Offices, dens, laptops, iPhones, iPads, Blackberrys, the whole big neural net.

- If I want to tell someone about the neat trick I pulled off ranking one of my blog posts at number 1 on Google for one of my favorite long-tail keywords, I need a member of the tribe.

- If I want to find a really good ecommerce vendor who can cashier payments, act nice with my email vendor and doesn't charge an arm and a leg, I need a member of my tribe, they'll know.

- If I want to get my blog performing better and looking more like a blog should, I need another blogger, that is, a member of the tribe.

- It's a tribe of reciprocity. People help each other more than in any other venture I've been a part of.

- It's a tribe of giving, because we've all drunk the Kool-Ade and have the giving mindset firmly in place as a first principle.

- It's a tribe of achievement. Members of this tribe are on a nonstop quest to better themselves, their income, their readership, their influence, their authority and their authenticity. As soon as they find out their one true niche.

- This tribe is empowered. I meet them in the self-publishing trenches, around the blogs, in forums, Linkedin discussions, over at the Third Tribe head-quarters, and all points in between.

- They are searching for meaning, for a place in the world, for the perfect domain name and a shot at immortality. We've grown up—or grown older—as the internet has matured.

- Twitter is the closest thing to a brain this tribe has. On Twitter I can meet and immediately identify other members of the tribe. They're informed. They're opinionated, if you don't mind. They're passionate about wanting passion in their lives.

- They tweet like songbirds, like telegraph machines, like drunken sailors. They tweet Rumi and Jung and Rodney Dangerfield in quick succession.

- They tweet hope, and outrage, and links to the 7 keys to a successful book launch.

- Tweets arrive at all hours of the day and night. Bored? Got two minutes while you wait for the carpool? The tweets are flowing, robust, demanding, selling, informing, whole novels in 140 characters.

And when I've had my fill, I can allow the public feed on Twitter, the tweets of all users in all languages from outposts of the tribe around the world to pour onto the screen in wave after wave of tweets. I can just stand there and let the languages, cultures, interests, concerns and endless endless human stories cascade over me in an ecstasy of info-flow.

Okay, now you know. Go play with your kids.

Two Things All Content Creators Can Do

There are only two things that are absolutely critical going forward:

Create Better Content—Whatever it is that we're doing is the content we deliver. It's a book, or an e-book. It's a performance or a recording. It's 3,000 words on Joe Biden. It's our content. This is the great equalizer, because it doesn't really matter who you are if your content is superior, amazing, sexy, intriguing, mind-blowing, the-first-of-its-kind or helpful. The content you created last year, last month, was great. Now make it better. Put more into it, make it more of whatever it is you're going for. We are using our content to identify our one true path, and claiming community in exactly the group that arrives to listen or hear or read or dance to that content. Our content performs some service, fills some need, scratches some itch. Enough itches to make it worthwhile creating the content. One thing we can do is create better content.

Create Paths to Content—How do people find our content? How can they be informed about our content? Is our content discoverable? It's 11:00 p.m., do you know where your Metadata are? Someone sits at a terminal typing into a search bar, looking for an answer–what question do you answer? Content without paths or bridges is an island. Knowing how to follow the pathways that search takes is central to a world in which the content of our cultures is being digitized. And the more content there is that's digitized and searchable, the more people there are to answer that question. How will you—your content—be found? One thing we can do is make our content discoverable.

Create better content, bring it to people's attention. Two things that will last a lifetime. Are you working on this too?

You Are the Market

How I Sold 10,000 Copies of My Self-Published Book

Jill and I were sitting around talking about friends and people we knew. I was trying to explain how the strange astrological system of personality types we were studying was complex enough to explain all the differences we were observing in our friends.

At one point Jill said to me, "How are people like me—new to this philosophy—supposed to learn all this? You've been talking about astrology, endocrine glands, mythology… I can't even keep track of it!" She looked exasperated.

"Well, just ask me if you have a question. How about that?" I said.

"That's no way to learn something this complicated. Isn't there anything written down?"

We looked at each other.

"Why don't you write it down, Joel, you know all this stuff. That way it would be available for anyone who comes along later, and it would be better than having to find someone to ask every time you had a question."

I had to admit Jill was right. It had just never occurred to anyone to write it all down. It was a study that hundreds of people were involved in, and which grew and changed, like a living teaching, over many years.

A Book is Born

Soon I was deep into the book that would become *Body Types*. What had started out as a little project to write down a few things about types had morphed into a full-scale manuscript that would take me over a year to put together.

Eventually I formed a publishing company—Globe Press Books—and published *Body Types* in both hardcover and softcover. I had an advantage at the beginning because I was a member of the group that had been developing this body type information, and I knew they would buy the book when it came out.

Here are the first two keys to selling your self-published book, and these are the exact things I did with *Body Types*:

First, *identify a market* for the book that you can easily advertise to. In my case, this was the group that we belonged to. I had membership lists with mailing addresses.

Second, *make that market an offer* they cannot refuse. I mailed to every address I could get, offering a special discount to people who ordered before the books were printed.

The great thing about this was that I collected enough money to pay for the initial print run of 2,500 books. I sold hundreds of copies in advance.

Since I had worked in book publishing and, at the time owned a graphic design studio in downtown Manhattan, I knew how to hire an editor, and how to create a book that looked as professional as any other book on the market. There had to be no indication that the book was self-published because of the strong prejudice against self-published books at the time.

Third, get professionals to *edit and design your book* so you can compete toe-to-toe with any other book on your shelf.

Find a Spot on the Shelf

Next we went after book reviews. This was crucial, since we couldn't afford to advertise.

Fourth, we mounted a large *book review campaign.* We mailed to several hundred media outlets, resulting in numerous reviews.

We then used the positive reviews to leverage ourselves in the larger network interested in spirituality and eastern teachings. We identified this as our natural market.

Fifth, we generated *press releases* using the reviews and used them to establish an identity in our niche.

But What's it All About?

Keep in mind that the biggest stumbling block we had with this book—and it was our only book for a couple of years—was that it was about a subject that no one had ever heard of. This is a daunting challenge that we addressed by taking our message to educational centers.

Sixth, we *obtained teaching assignments* at large alternative centers like the New York Open Center and the Omega Institute. Catalog mailings listing course descriptions and the title of the book multiplied our outreach through large scale network effects.

This all helped with the specialty bookstores that we needed to make the book a success. In this niche the specialty retailers were new age or human potential bookstores.

Seventh, we *personally sold each specialty retailer* we could identify, by mail and by phone, to convince them they had to have this book, the only one on its subject.

Back to Press

It took less than a year to sell the initial print run. We now had an account at Baker & Taylor, and a lot of people knew who we were. Because the book was unique, it established a place on the shelf of many bookstores. This is publishing gold. It means that, even though they may have only one or two copies on the shelf, when those copies sell, the bookstore *reorders the book* because they know there will be continuing demand.

We went back to press, concentrating on the $9.95 trade paperback (hey, this was the 1980s). Eventually sales, never that robust, slowed down. But they never stopped.

Eighth, we *listened to our market.* Readers only wanted the softcover so we abandoned the hardcovers, which had been a difficult sale anyway.

Eventually I started working on a new edition to incorporate the new research I had been doing, to add illustrations and a new forword by an well-regarded academic, Stanley Krippner. We put a new cover on the book, and issued the second edition with another print run of 2,500 softcovers. Since I now had a publishing company I had national distribution, and the book spread even farther.

The Ripples Widen As They Spread

I was invited to be a presenter at the First International Enneagram Conference at Stanford, and continued to give workshops after we moved to California. A couple of years later we went back to press for another 2,500 books.

Ninth, we continued to *leverage into bigger networks.* Each one helped amplify our message, and brought new readers to the idea of body types.

Body Types stayed in print continuously for 16 years. I didn't want to keep printing the book, and had handed over the distribution to another publisher, since I had closed our company. Eventually I let it go out of print.

Perhaps 10,000 books in 16 years doesn't sound like many to you, but it was profitable from publication date.

Now, thanks to print on demand and digital printing, I've been able to put *Body Types* back on the market with a new cover. It sits happily on its Amazon page, selling a steady trickle of books, ready for anyone who wants to discover it.

Think about what you know that others might find interesting. Know your niche and how to market to people with similar interests. Create a quality product. Take one step at a time and build credibility, leveraging into larger and larger networks. Take the long view, seeding success tomorrow by your actions today.

What Writers Need to Know Today

A friend wrote to me with the following question:

> What does the writer need to know or understand about the current status of publishing and the direction it is taking? What do you see for the future of publishing?

Here's my reply:

What writers need to know about the current state of publishing is that it is undergoing epochal change. Every part of the publishing industry is being affected by digitization, the rise of social media, and the unrelenting pressure on profits throughout the business.

Book publishing has been a tradition-bound business. The physical books themselves—where I've mostly been involved in publishing—have barely changed since the 15th century. They've only gotten easier to produce and consequently, cheaper. Technology has, until very recently, been in service to the way authors, publishers and booksellers have arranged the business of publishing.

In the meantime we continue to operate with the standard agent-author-publisher relationships, with the same consignment mentality in the bookselling world, in which all books are returnable for full credit. But the difference is that everyone knows this world is coming to an end, that most of the old structures will not survive the next change in publishing, and that the structures that do survive will be fundamentally different.

Today's writer, even if they are lucky enough to quickly get a book contract from one of our major publishers, needs to know:

How to find resources online—The abundance of resources online is simply staggering. From writing forums to free-writing websites, from agent blogs to writing webinars, you need to know how to find trustworthy sources of information.

How to build an author platform, online and off—Publishers are making more decisions based on the marketability of the author, rather than the book itself. An author with a huge online following simply represent less risk for a publisher to take on. Can you deliver a fan base along with a manuscript?

What their options are for publication—Many of the changes going on in publishing are due to the growing popularity of digital printing and print on demand distribution. This technology has put the ability to produce books into the hands of the ordinary person. Anyone sitting at a computer can now take a manuscript they've written and get very good looking softcover books a few days after putting in an order. And they can do this without spending any more than the wholesale cost of the books they buy. The explosion of self-publishing spurred by this technology is creating new types of publishers, new organizations, and new vitality and credibility for independent publishers. Each of the different paths you might choose to get published has its own risks and rewards, and you will have to know them before you can decide which path is right for you.

What kind of personality they want to project—Many writers have taken to blogging and other forms of social media with joy and enthusiasm, and they have multiplied their options for marketing their books and connecting with their own "tribe" of readers. Less gregarious writers may need to find a way to present themselves where they can attract potential readers. I don't mean to say that all writers are seeking readers. I'm saying that we write to be read, and whether you have 3 dedicated readers or 3,000, every writer has an investment in completing the loop, in being heard.

How to interact in social media—Every few months it seems that there are new ways to connect to people who share our interests. But the online environment has its own social norms, and spending time on social media pays dividends if you can make yourself heard in a way that interests, instructs, or entertains people. Many writers have their own websites, they blog regularly, and may have a presence on Facebook, Twitter, Linkedin, and other social media sites. Writers need to know how to establish themselves and foster long-term relationships within the context of a tsunami of tweets and status updates, to build connections that are lasting.

That e-books will bring an even bigger change to publishing—E-books, readable on computers, have been around for a long time. Amazon's Kindle has gotten people used to reading on a dedicated screen that tries to mimic a book. Now the Apple iPad looks ready to launch us into the next phase of the e-book revolution. Tablets and smartphones have increased the potential market for e-books by tens of millions of people. E-books give writers lots of options. Some authors are scared of the potential piracy of their works. Others are giving away books as fast as they can, or looking the other way at thosands of pirated books because it helps them build their brand. As digitization in all its forms spreads, e-books will eventually become the norm, and printed book will become special editions. I don't see printed books disappearing soon, but the eventual dominance of e-books in their place looks inevitable.

How to take the long view—The one thing that's certain is that we don't know what will happen next. Magazines want to quit cutting down trees entirely and find a home on something like the beautiful multi-media screen of the iPad. Although it's harder than ever to get an agent, more agents are approachable online than ever before. Sanity lies in the long view, in nurturing your own creativity above all. If you seek an audience, or publication, start putting yourself out for others to discover, and enjoy, now. You can't start too soon.

It seems to me the biggest obligation writers have is to the truth of their writing. The next most important thing for anyone who thinks about publication is getting educated. Start off with a good book, be open to new influences, and learn as much as you possibly can. Get involved in some of the hundreds of discussions going on. The process itself is its own reward.

Good Luck,

Joel

Why Self-Publishing is a Long-Tail Business

One of the most interesting stories in Dan Poynter's *Self-Publishing Manual* is how he became a book publisher. As an avid parachute jumper, Dan looked for but could not find a good basic manual for new people coming into his sport. Eventually he wrote one and sold it to his own and other parachuting clubs.

But what was interesting was that for some time Dan had no idea he had become a book publisher. He was just trying to fill a need, and that need could best be filled with an instructional manual. You can see that he used this same idea when he created his Self-Publishing Manual.

In a small way this story demonstrates why nonfiction publishing, including self-publishing, is often a long-tail phenomenon, and has been for a long time before the idea of the long tail was introduced by Chris Anderson in *Wired* magazine.

The Long Tail and the Niches

Let's back up for just a moment. Probably you've heard of the long tail, and it's certainly mentioned often enough in discussions of online business.

In the past, when it cost a lot to develop, produce and market products, businesses concentrated on blockbusters, or "hits" that would appeal to the widest possible audience. This capitalized on the "head" of the purchasing curve, where it was thought that most of the money was to be made.

As the cost to create and distribute products has fallen, largely due to digitization and the ability to market online, it has become apparent that the long tail of the purchasing curve contains potentially as much business as the head. Not only that, but each product in the tail, although it appeals to only a small segment of the population, is perfectly tailored to just that group of people. One thing this means is that if you can make those people aware of the product, they are much more likely to buy it.

The Long Tail and Nonfiction Publishing

In a sense, most nonfiction books are *marketing-driven* because they are often written for a specific niche. And the more specialized the book is, the more likely it is to find success within the group of people who are intensely interested in that niche.

When I was studying pizza making, for instance, I read almost every book I could find on baking artisinal pizza at home. This is a typical long-tail niche. Here's how it might look as you travel from the "head" to the "tail."

Imagine you are the publisher or self-publishing author of a book on serious home pizza baking. You want to find the keywords that people use to search for products of information you have to offer. You start at the top of the curve, at the big end of the funnel, and work you way down the long tail. Here's where it starts:

Cooking—this is the head of the curve, lots of people are interested in what is a huge market. But it's too big a designation for actual sales appeal.

Baking—here we've narrowed to only one aspect of cooking, coming down the purchase curve, but still in a very large category. I'm interested in pizza, not panettone or pastries.

Yeast Breads—at this point we start to enter the long tail, since this category is much more specific, and people looking here are much more likely to be interested in your books.

Flat breads—even farther down the tail, this subset of yeasted breads is of interest to only a small segment of the cooking/baking population, but they are highly engaged.

Pizza—although this particular tail ends here, another "long tail" begins with all books on making pizza and grows its own tail, with specialties such as deep-dish pizza baking, cormeal crust pizza baking, and so on.

Two Developments that Supercharged Nonfiction Niche Publishing

When the development and marketing of products was concentrated on the "hits," it was very expensive to create products and market them to a large enough population to ensure success. But two developments took the inherent "long tail" mindset of nonfiction publishing to a new level:

1. Internet marketing made it possible, for very little money, to attract just those people intensely interested in your niche. On discussion boards, blogs, forums and in discussion groups on community websites, people have congregated to talk about every possible activity

you can imagine, from the care of your tropical fish to digital photography, to genealogy, to pizza baking.

2.   Digital printing with print on demand distribution essentially eliminated most of the cost of getting a book into print.

These two developments alone have created a marketplace that rewards businesses and authors who can fulfill the needs of a small group of people. When you combine specialized information that experts in a field commonly posses with very targeted marketing and automated web delivery systems for either printed or electronic books, you've got a long tail marketing machine.

Authors, Get Your Keywords

Of course, the other technology that's made this targeting possible is *search*. The ever present search bar, usually a Google search bar, is an invitation to try to find an exact remedy.

A few years ago, after a pleasant walk in the woods with my son after Thanksgiving dinner, I came down with a nasty case of Poison Oak. It was from climbing over a dead tree, so I'll leave it to you to imagine exactly how much discomfort I was in.

I became a temporary member of a very small niche, people who wanted a cure for Poison Oak *right now* and were willing to pay for it. I eventually found a site, through Google search, for a cream guaranteed to cure what ailed me. A small vial was $45 and overnight shipping was available. This is the ultimate in long tail niche marketing, and it works.

As publishers, we can use this information to our advantage. Google and other search engines make available the actual search terms that people type into their search field. This powerful information is the statistics Google makes available on all the millions of keywords that people use to search the web.

An author who understands keywords, how they are used, and how to target the people who search on them, can go a long way toward making his nonfiction book a success.

Internet marketing combined with digital printing and print on demand distribution make nonfiction books perfect long-tail products.

Author Branding: The You That Is Everywhere

We've been told over and over again that to market effectively as self-publishers, we have to start building our author platform as early as possible.

But even before you start hammering together the platform that's going to support you and your book and your marketing efforts, you need to decide how you will brand yourself.

> Creating an author platform is vital for a new author's success, and creating a brand is the basis for the platform. You need to know what you are creating before you start!—*Joanna Penn*

What's that? You don't think of yourself as a box of Kleenex, a bar of soap, a transatlantic airline? That doesn't mean you don't need your own branding. It doesn't even mean you don't already have a brand of some kind if you're active in social media now.

Here's an example of a failure of corporate branding. When Fedex bought a ground delivery service, they only had to expand their brand a little to accommodate the idea of "secure trackable package delivery, express or ground."

But when Fedex bought Kinko's copy shops, they were reaching into unknown waters. Fedex is probably driven by the reality that many document transfers are now happening electronically, and Kinko's looked like a good diversification.

But they didn't keep Kinko's as Kinko's. They renamed it Fedex Kinko's which really makes no sense from a branding point of view. Then they dropped the Kinko's altogether.

Kinko's is a terrific and idiosyncratic brand of copy shops. "Kinko's" means one thing: copies and computer services 24 hours a day. What's Fedex doing in there? Now, they are stuck with a real branding problem. Outside our local Fedex/Office (Kinko's) is a small sign next to the door that says, "Kinko's." It's sad.

But as authors and self-publishers, what lessons can we learn to help with our own branding?

> We are CEOs of our own companies: Me Inc. To be in business today, our most important job is to be head marketer for the brand called You.—*Tom Peters*

Personal Branding: The You that is You

The idea of personal branding has been around for a while. Some people trace the idea back to an article in *Fast Company* magazine by legendary author and business writer Tom Peters.

Now, in the age of full-bore social media engagement, when it seems that every author has a Facebook page, a blog, a persona that represents them, the move to personal branding is stronger than ever.

> The Web makes the case for branding more directly than any packaged good or consumer product ever could. Here's what the Web says: Anyone can have a Web site. And today,

because anyone can ... anyone does! So how do you know which sites are worth visiting, which sites to bookmark, which sites are worth going to more than once? The answer: branding.—*Tom Peters*

The first thing you'll have to do is decide what your brand will be about.

Some Questions to Ask Yourself About Your Brand

What will be your brand?

- You as an author?
- Your book, as a solution to a problem?
- Your publishing company, as a provider of education or entertainment?

What Exactly Makes Up Your Brand?

You are branding yourself all the time—whether you know it or not. When you design your website or blog, when you pick out business cards, when you establish a persona through which you communicate with readers, other authors, book reviewers, you are branding yourself.

I'm a writer, a marketing consultant, a wife and mother, a business woman, a coach, a loyal friend, a passionate seeker of new challenges and also someone who loves the quiet solitude of reading on a beach. That abundance of choices and gifts can sometimes muddy the waters when I'm trying to define my "brand" to myself and to potential clients.— *Cindy Ratzlaff*

How intentionally you do these activities can have a major effect on your own brand. The most effective personal brands for authors are:

- Tightly focused
- Consistent
- In line with your subject matter

When I see the name John Grisham, immediately a brand leaps to mind—legal thrillers. Stephen King—horror stories. Robert Ludlum—action thrillers. Agatha Christie—genteel mysteries. Deepak Chopra—transcendental self-help. Are you thinking of your own examples? These are outstanding, consistent, tightly focused and congruent brands.

> Your external brand is how you project yourself to the world. There is an element of choice here. You can decide what to say or write in order to convey a certain image. Your projected image will influence what others think of you and how they might choose to interact with you. You may stumble upon this image accidentally, or you can deliberately target a specific type of image.—*Steve Pavlina*

When book buyers walk into a store—online or off—often they are looking for a brand rather than a book. "The new John Grisham" book. Booksellers (and Amazon's algorithms) offer possible books based on branding. "If you liked Malcolm Gladwell's *Tipping Point*, you might like Dan Ariely's *Predictably Irrational*."

This is true of many successful authors. When they want to write outside their usual style, they often do so under another name.

Here are two main reasons why personal branding is becoming a core part of our culture . . . First, we are all being judged all the time, even when we're sleeping (our online profiles are still up!). Second, we have to constantly sell our ideas to teachers, managers, venture capitalists, our friends and family, to make things happen in our lives. We have to convince them to take action.—*Dan Schwabel*

How do authors brand themselves? There are many ways. Your brand can be an expression of any part of your author presentation that ties people to your work. For instance, you could brand yourself by:

- Region—"Author of Western Adventure Stories"
- Genre—"Erotic Metaphysical Romances"
- Recurring Character—"Inspector Morris Mysteries"
- Style—"Easy to Read Books on Woodworking"
- Format—"1001 Ways to Manage your Career"
- Persona—"The Gen-Y Novelist With Attitude"
- Emotion—"The Feel-Good Books About Life's Little Problems"
- Notoriety—"The Trump Family of Casinos"

Really, any distinguishing characteristic can be the basis of a brand, if it's emphasized consistently as part of your presentation.

Branding in the World of Web 2.0

We have accounts everywhere online. But do you segregate your personal correspondence and postings from your author brand? Your fans from your friends?

I'm not proposing that you let the crowd dictate, or that you work hard to fit in. Far from it. I'm proposing that you know the impact your choices are having and act accordingly.—*Seth Godin*

Brands establish trust. I grew up in a family that used Colgate toothpaste, that was our brand. Why buy a new or different toothpaste, one we didn't know as well? We trusted our brand, and rewarded Colgate with our loyalty.

You want that trust from your readers and your community. If your brand is a sober, responsible and experienced tax advisor who writes books counseling people on the best way to save on taxes, how will your readers respond to those photos you posted of a wild weekend in Miami? This is the world we live in, it's just a reality.

Personal branding is leverage: once you know me, you start to build a relationship with me. Once we have a relationship, I can share even more with you. The more we share, the more likely we'll have other common interests down the road.—*Chris Brogan*

Branding matters if you rely on establishing trust and inspiring loyalty. From the way you dress to the way you leave comments on other people's blogs, you are constantly adding to your brand, and that's why consistency is so important.

So when it comes to platform building, first sit down and think about the brand you want to establish. How will you present yourself and your book to the world? How will you keep it consistent, tightly focused, and in line with your subject?

Figuring out your branding doesn't need to be complicated, but it does need to be focused. I'm not talking about the kind of branding that requires hours of logo development. I'm not even talking about a brand that's necessarily original. Yes, you want to be unique, but the key isn't doing something no one else is doing, the key is doing it better.—*Penny Sansevieri*

After you've answered these questions you'll be more prepared for your platform building. And to really find out how others see you, ask them. You're likely to receive some eye-opening feedback and advice. But if you care about the impression you're making and how it reflects on your work, this is some of the most important listening you will ever do.

Author Platform: What Are You Waiting For?

A famous and often-repeated piece of advice to writers is: The time to start working on your author platform is three years before your book is published.

I've repeated this to several clients, and it usually leaves them staring blankly into space. And yet there is a great deal of wisdom in this statement, and a radical remaking of the work of an author.

Many writers have no interest in getting involved with selling their work, or doing promotion. This article isn't for them.

That's because a lot of writers have realized that it's become their responsibility to market their books. Publishers are asking them to do it, authors are routinely submitting marketing plans along with their book proposals. I spoke to a book shepherd recently who told me they were hard at work on a 20-page marketing plan for an author-client.

And it doesn't really matter if you write fiction or nonfiction. The new reality is that you are in charge of finding, and cultivating, your own readership. Of course, if you are successful enough at it, you will acquire a big publisher complete with a marketing and advertising department to broadcast your efforts into a much larger space.

It's a Matter of Community

Where I live in northern California, I partcipate in several communities. There's the community of families at our son's school. There's the community in our neighborhood, where we plan street improvements and train for emergencies together. There's the community of self-publishers, independent publishers and soon-to-be-publishers of which I'm a member.

In each case, within our geographic area, we form communities of interest.

For writers, the internet and its various social media—taken broadly to mean any method for interacting with other people on an equal footing—are how we find our communities of interest. Some of the tools we use are:

- Author blogs
- Writing forums
- Other people's blogs
- Facebook groups and pages
- Linkedin discussion groups
- Twitter #discussions and lists
- Specialized social groups like Ning networks

A rational person understands that he cannot do all of these activities at once. What's needed is a plan or strategy because, faced with all the possibilities, the normal human reaction is to put it off, and do nothing.

Unfortunately, this may not be the best solution.

The Time for Waiting is Over

In a recent article, "Audience Development: Critical to Every Writer's Future," Jane Friedman of *Writer's Digest* said:

> Getting a book published does NOT equate to readership. You must cultivate a readership every day of your life, and you start TODAY. Your readers will not be interested in reading just one book; they will be interested in everything and anything you do—and that includes interacting with you online. Audience development doesn't happen over-night (or even in 6 months or a year)—and it's a process that continues for as long as you want to have a readership. It shouldn't be delayed, postponed, or discounted for one minute.

Taking one step, setting up a blog for instance, can start you on the road to finding the community whose common interest is you and your writing. Your audience is out there, but they don't know it yet. It's your job to find those readers who are just waiting for a writer like you to come along. They will like you a lot. Some will be insanely devoted. But you have to reach out.

Getting a domain name, signing up for a hosting account, and installing blogging software takes about 10 minutes. And that's the hard way.

If we are really writers, if we are writers who want readers, the closing of the circle of our own creativity, then let's write, and find out who reads. That will be the beginning of our community, and it will grow from there. If we are going to be writers for a long time—and I believe it's a chronic condition—why not start now?

Resources, Tools, Freebies are Everywhere

Even a casual search online will reveal lots of resources, links, free reports, strategies and information that can help get you going. My suggestion: don't pay for any programs, tutorials, or anything else until you've gotten all you can from the free resources available. There's a whole education out there just waiting for you.

The resources are vast. All they require is your participation, your intention to act now.

Writing and Community-Building: The Writer's New Job Description

In this new world, writers who want to write and market their books will find their job is now two-fold: writing, and building community around their writing. Find the social media that appeal to you, share your work, interact with your readers, reach out to the wider reading world in different formats, and start now building the community that will support and nurture you on your writing path.

Sources

The Secret to Successful Self-Publishing
Chip MacGregor, The Competitive Analysis
http://chipmacgregor.typepad.com/main/2010/01/the-competitive-analysis.html

What Does It Take to Make A Publishing Company?
Edward Nawotka, Publishing Perspectives
http://publishingperspectives.com/2010/09/when-does-a-self-publisher-constitute-a-publishing-company/

John T. Reed, John T. Reed Publishing
http://johntreed.com/

Does Book Design Really Matter?
Morris Rosenthal, Self-Publishing 2.0
http://www.fonerbooks.com/cornered.htm

Jane Friedman, Publishing Passion
http://www.janefriedman.com/

Dummies.com
http://www.dummies.com/how-to/content/avoiding-selfpublishing-mistakes.html

Walt Shiel, Slipdown Mountain Publications, View from the Publishing Trenches blog
http://waltshiel.com/

Lyn Miller-Lachmann, Blogger and Editor, *Multicultural Review*
http://web.mac.com/lynml/Site/Home.html

Denise Hamilton, Ink Tree, Ltd.
http://www.inktreemarketing.com/

Dan Holloway, danholloway.wordpress.com
http://www.danholloway.wordpress.com/

Rise of the Content Creators
Mark Coker, Smashwords
http://blog.smashwords.com/2010/04/smashwords-ebooks-ipad-ebook-publishing.html

JA Konrath, A Newbie's Guide to Publishing
http://jakonrath.blogspot.com/

Ken Auletta, The *New Yorker*
http://www.newyorker.com/reporting/2010/04/26/100426fa_fact_auletta

Frank Bell, *Entrepreneur*
http://www.microsoft.com/smallbusiness/resources/marketing/advertising-branding/The-Rise-of-User-Generated-Content.aspx#TheRiseofUserGeneratedContent

James Woollam, Futurebook
http://www.futurebook.net/content/view-ebook-length

Michael Learmont, *Advertising Age* Online
http://adage.com/article?article_id=144334

Self-Publishing Pro and Con(temptuous)
Rachelle Gardner, Rants and Ramblings, Think Hard Before Self-Publishing
http://cba-ramblings.blogspot.com/2010/03/think-hard-before-self-publishing.html

Alan Rinzler, The Book Deal, How Self-Publishing Can Lead to a Real Book Deal
http://www.alanrinzler.com/blog/2010/03/11/how-self-publishing-can-lead-to-a-real-book-deal/

EBooks Today: Futility or Utility?
April Hamilton
http://www.aprilhamilton.com/

Craig Mod, @craigmod, Books in the Age of the iPad
http://craigmod.com/journal/ipad_and_books/

Less Expensive, Bite-Sized, Available for Take-Out: The Book of the Future
Mark Barrett, Ditchwalk
http://www.ditchwalk.com/2010/02/16/open-source-epub-vs-adobe-pdf/

The Problem With "E-Books"
E.M. Ginger, 42-line.com
http://www.thebookdesigner.com/2010/01/e-m-ginger-on-digitizing-the-art-of-the-book/

Author Branding: The You That Is Everywhere
Joanna Penn: How to Discover and Build Your Author Brand
http://www.thecreativepenn.com/2009/08/03/how-to-discover-and-build-your-author-brand/

Dan Schwabel: An Introduction to the World of Personal Branding
http://www.personalbrandingblog.com/an-introduction-into-the-world-of-personal-branding/

Chris Brogan: My Best Advice About Personal Branding
http://www.chrisbrogan.com/my-best-advice-about-personal-branding/

Cindy Ratzlaff: Five Secrets to Creating Brand: You
http://cindyratzlaff.com/blog/personal-branding/five-secrets-to-creating-brand-you/

Steve Pavlina: Personal Branding
http://www.stevepavlina.com/blog/2008/02/personal-branding/

Tom Peters: The Brand Called You
http://www.fastcompany.com/magazine/10/brandyou.html

Seth Godin: Personal Branding in the Age of Google
http://sethgodin.typepad.com/seths_blog/2009/02/personal-branding-in-the-age-of-google.html

Penny Sansevieri: Don't Be An Expert, Be A Filter (Secrets To Selling More Books)
http://www.amarketingexpert.com/dont-be-an-expert-be-a-filter-secrets-to-selling-more-books/

Want More?

The ideas in this book were developed in the articles I write for my blog. You are invited to visit the blog and find out what we're talking about now. Sign up for a free subscription and you won't miss. You can also participate in the conversations going on there with the community of writers, designers, self-publishers and internet entrepreneurs who you'll meet there.

You'll also find more publications and training tools to help authors create better, more profitable books, and to help them market those books. These include:

- Reports—My series of subject-specific reports, the *Self-Publisher's Quick & Easy Guides,* is growing. Get answers to specific questions with downloads in PDF, Kindle and ePub formats.

- Teleseminars—In-depth discussions of book design and marketing ideas for self-publishers and how they affect your profitability. These audio downloads offer lots of detailed advice.

- Webinars—Presentations including *Author Blogging 101* and *Book Design for Self-Publishers* add a video component for multimedia learning. Downloadable movie files for at-home study.

- Books—Watch for more titles in 2011

See you there!

http://www.TheBookDesigner.com

070.5

JAN 1 1 2012

AUG 06 2012

BASEMENT

CPSIA information can be obtained at www.ICGtesting.com
Printed in the USA
LVOW061657121211

259058LV00002B/34/P

9 780936 385112